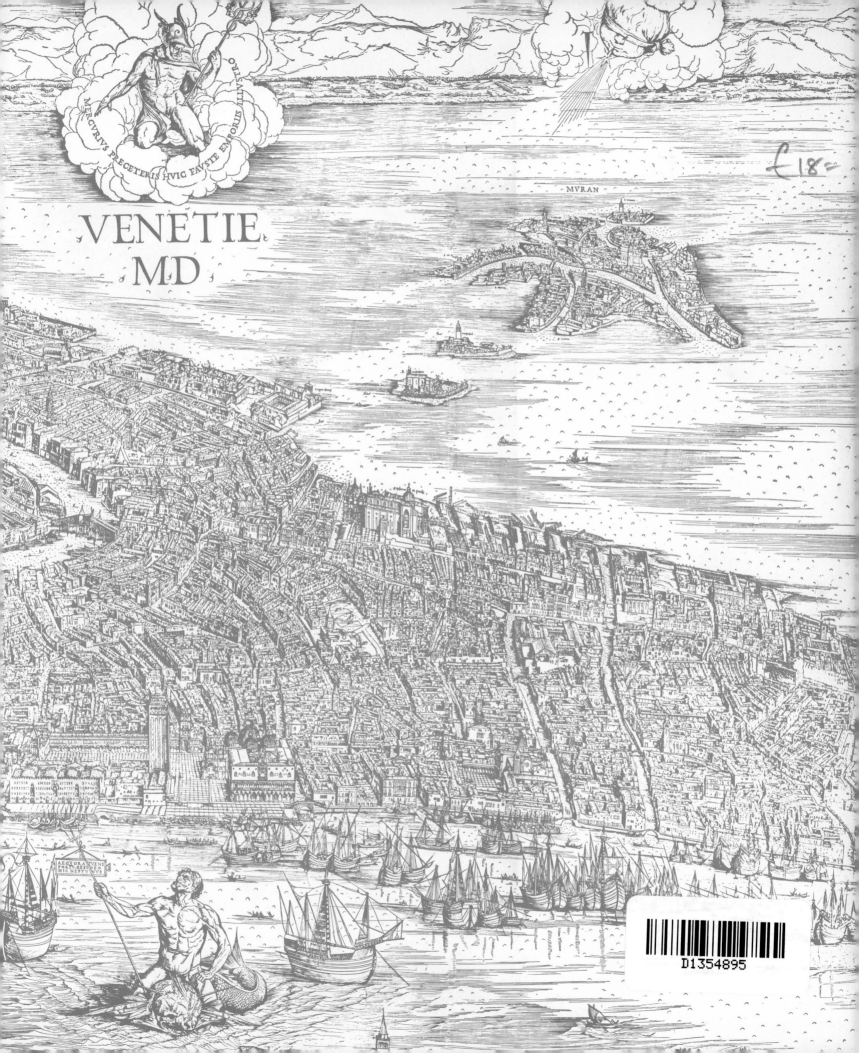

PALACES OF VENICE

PALACES OF VENICE

by PETER LAURITZEN
and ALEXANDER ZIELCKE

Phaidon

For Rose

This book was designed and produced by
BLACKER CALMANN COOPER LTD, *London*

PHAIDON PRESS LIMITED
Littlegate House, St Ebbe's Street, Oxford

First published 1978
© 1978 by Blacker Calmann Cooper Ltd

ISBN 0 7148 1714 7

Printed in West Germany by F. Bruckmann KG, Munich
Typesetting by Composing Operations Ltd, Tunbridge Wells

Contents

Contents

Preface

The UNESCO report of 1969 points out that at least 397 palaces in the city of Venice are of sufficient artistic or architectural interest to merit restoration and preservation. I have chosen to treat briefly only forty-five of them. They have been selected according to architectural criteria save in two cases, where the interiors are of particular interest in illustrating Venetian taste. Although I have attempted to trace the general development of Venetian domestic architecture, this book is aimed at the general reader and interested visitor, not at the scholar of Venice's architectural history. Since Fontana began writing in instalments published over one hundred and fifty years ago, there has been no general survey of the city's palaces save for the book prepared by Thomas Okey in English at the beginning of this century; and lacking an illustrated guide, the visitor to the city is often bewildered by the number of old houses he sees. Of course, the palaces of a city as unique as Venice should be seen in context. But it is my belief that many of them are beautiful in themselves and illustrate the peculiarities of the context in which they were created, and that they stand up well to examination in isolation. I have tried to make these houses memorable by an anecdotal approach to their histories. The Venetian patriciate was such a peculiarly cohesive unit, and the houses they built so strongly reflect not only their individual tastes but also their relationship to the city they governed, that I hope my approach will seem the right one.

In my introduction I speak of the difficulty of Venetian historiography; for this book I have relied on standard sources and my own first-hand experience of the houses. Fontana, Tassini, and the guide-books of Lorenzetti, the Touring Club Italiano, and Reclam have often been the source of frustrating contradictions, but are nonetheless indispensable. Litta and Barbaro provide endless genealogical information as well as confusion, and one must be careful not to lose sight of the woods for the genealogical trees. Among the principal monograph studies I have found useful are those of Giorgia Scattolin on the early period, recent monographs on Sanmicheli, Sansovino, and Longhena, and a general study of the Venetian Baroque by Elena Bassi. For the Gothic period Edoardo Arslan's study is the most recent and comprehensive. In addition I have consulted various specialized studies and biographies of individual Venetians. A list of the relevant literature as well as suggestions for general reading will be found in the select bibliography.

This book could not have been realized without the collaboration of Alexander Zielcke, who has captured the essence of the buildings in his fine

2. Looking across campo San Vio and the Grand Canal to Palazzo Barbaro

photographs. Our partnership, and indeed in many ways the very idea of this book, owes much to John Calmann, our editorial consultant. Special thanks are due to many Venetian friends who showed an interest in the project, made helpful suggestions and offered us hospitality.

Particular thanks should go to Barone Rubin de Cervin Abrizzi and his son Alessandro; to Mrs Ralph Curtis; to Contessa Giustinian; to Baronessa Elsa Treves de'Bonfili and to Conte Volpi di Misurata for allowing us to photograph their houses.

We should also like to thank Arch. Renato Padoan, the Superintendent of Monuments, Prof. Francesco Valcanover, the Superintendent of the Galleries, and Contessa Eleana Chiappini of the Correr Museum for their kind help. Our thanks also go to Bill Hughes and Peter Herzog for their invaluable assistance.

For my own part I should like to acknowledge my debt to the late Canon Victor Stanley, who introduced me to Venice and who first interested me in the study of buildings and their history. But even with all the help I here gratefully and humbly acknowledge, little or none of my work would have been realized had it not been for my wife, Rose, to whom the whole is dedicated.

P. L. LAURITZEN
Venice 1977

Introduction

The origins of Venice are shrouded in the mists of her lagoon and embalmed in thousands of pages of purple prose. The historiographers and propagandists of the Most Serene Republic are partly to blame, but the enduring heritage of paradox and enigma which this ancient gateway to the East had received from Byzantium confounds the serious historian at every turn. We know little enough of her original inhabitants, though the date of the election of their first doge, or duke, in AD697 has been given the sanction of tradition. That year gives a nice symmetry to the Republic's long history – the Venetian state collapsed exactly one thousand one hundred years later with the arrival of Napoleon's troops in 1797. In the span of the city's history as a sovereign state exactly 120 doges were elected and crowned with the curious ducal bonnet, or *cornù*; and in the eighteenth century it was observed that the frieze of the Great Council chamber, where the ducal portraits were hung, contained only 120 places. Membership of the Maggior Consiglio (Great Council) was closed to the citizenry and made the hereditary prerogative of the aristocracy in the year 1297. Thus Venetian history can be conveniently, if perhaps too neatly, divided between the dates 697, 1297, and 1797. Needless to say, only the last date is securely documented.

3. San Vidal and Santo Stefano from Palazzo Cavalli-Franchetti

The life-span of the Most Serene Republic was remarkable. As a city-state which was the capital of a 'ducal republic', its peculiar form of government lasted longer than the Holy Roman Empire or the Empire of Byzantium, founded by Constantine the Great and brought to an inglorious end during the Fourth Crusade by the Venetians themselves. Most historians of Venice are concerned with the years between 697 and 1797, for hardly anything is known for certain about the earlier centuries of life on the lagoon islands. When the Republic's historiographers tell us that the city was 'founded' on 25 March AD421 at noon, or that Saint Mark the Evangelist had visited the lagoon islands even earlier, one can only respectfully repeat these legends sanctioned by Venice's millennial history and pass on. Its foundation in the fifth century makes Venice a youngster among the great cities of Europe. The Roman armies, who established military bases at Florence, Paris, and London, by-passed the lagoon islands and, despite the patronage of Saint Mark, Venice cannot claim any documented connection with the apostolic or palaeochristian centuries of European history. Even its oldest surviving buildings are of very recent date. The visitor today sees virtually nothing of the period of the Republic's greatest power, but only what economic

Introduction

historians would describe, with the accuracy of hindsight, as the period of her decline and even decadence.

We catch a glimpse of the earliest Venetians in a letter written by Cassiodorus in the late sixth century. He addresses the military tribunes who then represented the Emperor among these descendants of untold generations of natives, who eked out a living by fishing or working the salt pans their ancestors had shored up on the shoals of the lagoon. Cassiodorus sweetens his demand for the usual tribute with a laudatory and apparently first-hand description of their way of life and their habitations. 'There lie your houses built like sea-birds' nests, half on sea and half on land . . . made not by Nature but created by the industry of man. For the solidity of the earth is secured only by wattle-work; and yet you fear not to place so frail a barrier between yourselves and the sea. Your inhabitants have fish in abundance. There is no distinction between rich and poor; the same food for all; the houses all alike; and so envy, that vice which rules the world, is absent here. All your activity is devoted to the salt-works, whence comes your wealth . . . From your gains you repair your boats which, like horses, you keep tied up at your house doors.' This letter has often been quoted and many of Cassiodorus's remarks could serve as the basis for many valid generalizations about Venice, her inhabitants, and their houses. Although none of the primitive wooden houses of the earliest Venetians has survived, there still exist clues as to what they may have been like. The *cavane*, or boat shelters of the lagoon fishermen, still have reed-thatched roofs raised above the water on the same larch poles that were sunk for the piling foundations of the palace in the city. A platform under the pitched roof provides storage for the fishing nets and, as in Cassiodorus's day, when they provided the fisherman as well as his boat with shelter, they are built half in the water and half on the mud-flat 'land' of the lagoon islands.

The wood for the pilings originally came from the *lido*, the thin littoral stretch of soil and sand that separates the lagoon from the Adriatic sea. The abundance of building material available on the lido probably explains why the refugees from the mainland first settled there. Even before the arrival of the mainlanders, the natives of the lagoon had established an export trade in timber and salt. Their trade routes followed the Brenta, Sile, and Piave rivers, which at that time flowed into the lagoon. This trade probably introduced them to the art of brick-firing as practised by the inhabitants of the mainland: descendants not only of prehistoric tribes, but also of Caesar's legionaries who had been allotted land in the Empire's tenth military district, Venetia-Histria. Earlier than written record can document, brick and wood-piling were essential elements of Venetian building and remain so to this day. Stone, which never became an essential element, was undoubtedly introduced by the predominantly Romanized mainlanders who fled from the onslaught of the barbarians at the break-up of the Roman empire.

The history of the successive barbarian invasions of Northern Italy is complex, and the eventual destruction of many Roman mainland settlements, fortifications, and towns, took centuries to accomplish. The earliest refugees did not arrive with columns, capitals, and statuary in their vans. Indeed, modern scholarship suggests that at first they did not settle permanently in the safety of the lagoon, but returned to their mainland homes as soon as the danger was past. It was only later, after successive invasions had threatened their sense of security on the mainland, and the Longobardi had wrought widespread destruction, that the demoralized Romans sought permanent asylum on the lido. Over decades of settlement and re-settlement, they brought stone fragments from their temples and public buildings to their new sanctuary. Because of their rarity, value, and sentimental associations, these bits and pieces of carved and inscribed stone followed the migration of the first refugees from the lido to their eventual resting place in the buildings of the innermost islands. These stones testify to the very slow and gradual nature of a migration so summarily described: inscribed stones that once adorned pagan temples on the mainland are still to be seen in the foundations of the oldest Venetian churches.

The variety of stone the Romans brought with them reflects the riches of the cities they left behind: Altinum, Patavium (modern Padua), Eraclea, Aquileia, and Concordia; but for the most part their stone was the hard, white marble quarried locally in the province of Histria: *pietra d'Istria* or Istrian stone. By the time the first doge was elected in 697, the Venetian repertoire of building materials was complete: piling and timber from the lido and mainland forests, deep-red brick moulded in the classic Roman dimensions, and milky white Istrian stone. Of course, only few refugee families could afford to build houses of these solid, expensive and rare imported materials; most continued to build in wood. Those who could afford to build strongholds for their families were, in many cases, the ancestors of those who built the palaces discussed below. Numerous tombstones, inscriptions, and documents of the Roman imperial period link Venetian family names to their Roman ancestry more convincingly than many of the elaborate genealogies drawn up for the Renaissance princes of Rome herself.

Though the arrival of rich families from the mainland undoubtedly introduced the concept of aristocracy among the fisherfolk and native sailors of the lagoon, the idea was probably little codified until well after the early elections of their first leaders by universal suffrage. By the early ninth century, when Charlemagne had defeated the Lombards in Northern Italy and had recognized and treated with Venetian leaders, and his son Pepin had attacked the lagoon-dwellers in an attempt to force their allegiance to his western realm, Venice was firmly allied with the eastern Roman Empire. The Venetian doges were in reality vassals of the Exarch of Ravenna, who represented the Emperor of Byzantium. Thus the Venetian aristocracy came to be organized not on feudal western lines, but in terms of commercial wealth and expertise in matters of state that prevailed at Constantinople. As is well known, Venice's commercial ties with the East and her political affiliation with the Byzantine empire influenced her architecture – the basilica of San Marco, the doge's palatine chapel as it then was, is the most obvious

Introduction

example. For domestic architecture, Byzantine influence can be seen in palaces existing in Venice today, particularly in the use of stilted arches, basket capitals, paterae, and other carved stonework details.

The Venetians early repudiated their token vassalage to the emperor at Constantinople, but commercial success and statesmanship continued to characterize their palace-building class. As the concept of an aristocracy began to be more clearly defined, certain peculiarities emerged. From the earliest days of the Republic until its collapse at the end of the eighteenth century, there was hardly a trace of primogeniture within the patrician families: no individual was considered head of the family by reason of lineal descent. One member of a numerous clan might be thought of as their leader, but in almost every case his primacy was due to conspicuous wealth, power, or position within the government. In the succeeding generation, token leadership of the clan might pass to another branch of the family. Lack of primogeniture meant that a patrician's fortune did not necessarily go to his eldest son; it might instead be divided between all his male offspring, or might pass to only two of five sons, depending on the testator's dispositions. Surprisingly few sons of a patrician Venetian married, and often the eldest entered the Church. With help from a rich and powerful father, such a son might gather enough benefices and ecclesiastical offices to establish himself financially, and consequently be left only a token legacy when his father died. His younger brothers, or perhaps only the one who had married, would be left the substantial portion of the estate. In general, only a patrician's own sons received the bulk of his wealth and properties. His nephews, if their father was rich or successful, would constitute another branch of the family. To distinguish themselves from their collaterals, the members of such a branch often added to the family name the name of the parish where they built their palace.

There was never in Venice any single palace that could be considered the family seat. Over the centuries, branches of the great Contarini family built well over twenty-five palaces in the city. Many of these are still known as Palazzo Contarini, differentiated only by the name of the parish or by some characteristic of the building itself: the Contarini degli Scrigni (of the money chests), the Contarini della Porta di Ferro (of the iron door), the Contarini del Bovolo (of the cork-screw staircase), the Contarini delle Figure (of the figures). Many of the palaces originally built for the Contarini are now disguised by the names of later owners. Thus, the Palazzo Contarini dal Zaffo at San Vio is now known as the Palazzo de Polignac, and the Contarini house at Santa Sofia is called the Ca' d'Oro. It was quite common for a patrician family to buy and move into a house that had been built for another family, or for a palace to be divided between two or more families through inheritance or purchase. Thus, there are only two families left in Venice that still inhabit the house built for their ancestors, though there are several palaces built for other families that are still lived in by the descendants of patricians who purchased them in the seventeenth century. In every case, it is important to

4. Late fifteenth-century spiral staircase (Bovolo) and loggias, unique in Venice, at the late Gothic Palazzo Contarini del Bovolo

remember that the Venetian palace was essentially a single family unit. Brothers, uncles, aunts, cousins, and other relatives did not live under the same roof, as they did in Florence or Rome, where a wing or a suite of secondary rooms was set aside for their use.

Despite the ramification and apparent fragmentation of the patrician family, a family spirit not unlike that of the clan prevailed, and much of the Republic's legislation was aimed at preventing the predominance of any single family branch or clan. On the larger scale, the entire patriciate was like a family, though it is significant that blood ties and loyalties were less important than commercial partnerships or service to the state. Investment partnerships, called *colleganze*, were often made between brothers, or between uncles and nephews, or included a wide circle of relations, or were even made outside the family altogether. There was no pattern to these joint ownership ventures, though a patrician's sons and brothers were often his agents abroad or captained the galleys he leased from the state. The Venetian galley was built in the Arsenal under government supervision. It was owned by the state and was available to the merchant patrician or his *colleganza* by franchise, but it was also equipped as a fighting vessel. The merchant fleet and the Venetian navy were virtually one and the same. Since every male Venetian noble over the age of twenty-six was obliged to serve at least on the Great Council, the deliberations and legislation of the government were naturally concerned with preserving the prosperity of its members' trading ventures. Commercial enterprise and service to the state were, for the Venetian patrician, inextricably bound.

In the fourteenth century, the population of Venice was approximately 100,000 people. There were about one hundred patrician families, though only twenty or thirty could have been considered 'great' families. From these hundred families there were approximately five hundred men serving the state in administrative posts or voting in the councils of the government. The government controlled outright monopolies of both salt and grain. It also controlled the staple rights over the upper two-thirds of the Gulf of Venice, as the Adriatic sea was then known. Staple rights meant that cargoes carried by any nation's merchant fleet to ports within the designated area were subject to Venetian tax and commercial regulations. As a result, cargoes were often sent from the port in question to Venice itself for the final sale. The staple rights, which effectively encouraged the shipper to use the port of Venice for all his transactions, were enforced by the navy, but the port city itself, though abiding by Venetian commercial restrictions, might owe its political allegiance to another government.

Within her mainland territories, Venice's policy was imperialist. Mainland cities in the Republic did retain a certain autonomy though their rôle in filling the coffers of the *Dominante* was never overlooked. In the history of architecture, the mainland expansion belongs more to the story of the villas of the Veneto than to that of the palaces of Venice, but the patrician palace-builders did, especially in later centuries, derive a great deal of their wealth from their mainland possessions. And of course, the state, and thus indirectly the patriciate, prospered with the control of overland and river trade. The trade routes of Venetia led mainly to Germany and Central Europe, and the trade fairs held in Venetian territory were also a source of considerable revenue for the government.

Venice's empire in the Levant was a compilation resulting from her policies in the Gulf and those of her mainland administration. Her principal possessions, Cyprus, Crete, and Corfu, enjoyed semi-autonomous government, whereas smaller islands were often held in fief by a single Venetian family. But the backbone of her far-flung and amorphous empire was the merchant colonies established in the ports and coastal cities of the Near East. These colonies throve under the protection of the Venetian fleet and the privileges granted them by the emperors at Constantinople. The merchants were often either patricians themselves or the agents of *colleganze* organized by patricians in Venice. Thus the vast fortunes made in the Levant enriched the *Dominante* as well as her patrician class.

With so much power and wealth in the hands of so few, much legislation was enacted to circumscribe the power of families or individuals. The most obvious target of such legislation was the doge himself. A new doge was sworn into his life-long office after he had agreed to abide by a *promissione*, or list of promises, drawn up by a committee on his predecessor's death. The *promissione* anticipated possible abuses of the ducal offices and power, and over the centuries it became ever more restrictive so that guide-book historians and even many serious scholars have described the ducal powers as effectively reduced to nought and the man himself as a voiceless, splendidly plumed *rara avis* imprisoned in the proverbial gilded cage. This was not quite the case. The doge always enjoyed immense prestige among the Venetians and in the councils of the state, and he was one of the few individuals actually allowed to propose legislation – a function otherwise performed by committee. With his long experience of the intricate checks and balances of the constitution and bureaucracy, he would consult his councillors and the various councils he presided over, and he hardly ever made proposals contrary to their advice. But the patriciate remained ever alert to the possibility of a doge's abuse of power or even dynastic ambitions. For that reason, one of the most frequently renewed clauses was that none of the male members of the doge's immediate family should hold high office during his reign. Fear of a ducal cabal led to the clause whereby all the doge's private correspondence was opened and read by the Council of Ten. Many other aspects of his private life were under similar scrutiny and restriction by the government. But he was not the only patrician subject to such restrictive legislation. The *Maggior Consiglio* and its upper house, the Senate – in other words the patriciate as a whole – enacted many laws aimed at preventing the formation of powerful family cliques. With a typical Venetian thoroughness, these laws often covered the minutiae of the patrician's life. For example, he was forbidden to sponsor at baptism another patrician's child; godfatherhood, it was felt, added to matrimonial ties, would result in a mafia-like 'family' of power and protection.

The great wealth and consequent power of a patrician family could not have been reduced by the government without indirectly weakening the state itself, but restrictions could be placed on a too conspicuous display of that wealth. Hence the sumptuary laws, the effect of which can be seen in Venice today. For example, the competitive display of wealth expended by patricians on their principal form of transport was interpreted by the government as a possible source of overbearing pride in some cases and of debt and ruin in others. Anxious to avoid either for its members, the Maggior Consiglio decreed that all gondolas should be painted black. The frequent passage and renewal of similar sumptuary laws shows, in fact, that the very rich constantly managed to circumvent the restrictions. In the case of gondolas, the boat itself was painted black, but it was often given an overall gala dress of coloured velvet, with a length of that rare and expensive material trailing in the water from the stern.

Sumptuary laws also attempted to curb the lavish display affected by patricians at the marriage of their daughters. The size of the dowry early came under control, as did the number of courses to be served at the bridal dinner. Once married, the patrician lady found that her dress and ornaments were subject to government regulation. Only a certain number of pearls could be worn or a certain yardage of brocade or velvet. Venetian fashions were often the subject of comment in the writings of visiting foreigners and not least curious were considered the pattens, the tall, stilted shoes worn by the ladies. These shoes, which caused the Venetian lady to shuffle slowly along, holding the heads of two maidservants, were not worn to keep her feet dry on the rare days of the *acqua alta*, but rather permitted her to wear greater lengths of rare materials and thus circumvent the laws that had curtailed her train.

The sumptuary laws also affected the palaces. Venetian domestic architecture was basically eclectic and conservative. By comparison with his Roman or Florentine counterpart, the Venetian patrician was relatively uninterested in architectural innovation, and the government's enforcement of conformity hardly affected palace design. But the state often restricted the size of palaces, such as the Palazzo Pisani at Santo Stefano, which was thought too grand even for one of the city's richest banking families. Certain decorative or structural details were the object of legislation. Unlike the Florentine palace, no Venetian house was allowed to have projecting eaves that might darken the narrow *calli*. Nor could a Venetian palace roof be decorated with balustrades and ornamental statuary after the Roman Baroque fashion. The only ornament permitted above the cornice was the old-fashioned chimney or else twin obelisks, and these latter embellishments were only allowed on the houses of high officials in the navy.

The sumptuary laws concerning the decoration of palace interiors were more comprehensive. Patrician magnificence and pretension were curbed by laws restricting the yardage of silks or brocades used to cover the walls of

5. The marble-encrusted façade of Palazzo Contarini-Polignac

Introduction

rooms and the number and size of tapestries hung. It is interesting to note that while wall hangings were the object of numerous regulations, furniture, numbers of servants, or the quantity of gold and silver plate were not. During the Middle Ages and the Renaissance, wall hangings represented luxury more than did furniture, which was sparse and often moved from room to room. Servants were numerous in a rich man's house, but contemporary accounts suggest that they lived informally with their masters until a greater formality became fashionable in later centuries. The display of silver and gold at times of family festivities, such as weddings, was restricted, but the amount the noble could own was not; plate represented the family's uninvested capital.

Finally, the egalitarian tone of the legislation regarding the patriciate produced two other peculiarities, which lasted until the fall of the Republic in 1797. The Venetian noble never bore a title in Venice. In personal address and in documents, obsequious-sounding courtesies did begin to appear – 'illustrissimo', 'eccellentissimo', etc. – but these were never used as titles and the Venetian aristocrat was officially distinguished simply by the initials N.H. and N.D., *Nobil Homo* and *Nobile Donna*. In many cases, he had the right to bear feudal titles granted by the Latin Emperor of the East, the Emperor of Byzantium, or one of their vassals, such as the Lusignan king of Cyprus, but the use of these titles was forbidden in the Republic itself. Despite the lack of hierarchical distinctions, the Venetian patrician was granted the highest precedence in the courts of Europe, though the malicious sneered at these proud nobles as mere fishermen and merchants. The other curiosity peculiar to Venice, and in the same paradoxically egalitarian spirit, was the fact that until the fall of the Republic none of the Venetian palaces were called palaces. There was only one palace in Venice, the Palazzo Ducale: all the rest, no matter how grand, were mere *case*, houses. The old form still survives in its abbreviated form in such cases as Ca' Rezzonico, Ca' Foscari, and Ca' d'Oro. Otherwise, these houses have all become known as *palazzi* – even some of the humblest and least significant. And after the fall of the Republic, too, the patricians forgot all their state-oriented scruples and accepted almost to a man the resounding, but historically empty titles offered them by their new masters: they became counts of the Austrian Empire.

The historian of Venice is plagued by all sorts of ironies: such as writing about an aristocracy that governed a city-state along republican and even welfare state lines; that enjoyed the prestige of ancient lineage yet had no primogeniture; that used no titles, and based the rank of its members not on the extent of their feudal domain, but on their enterprise as merchants and their talents as bureaucrats. Not the least of such ironies is the title of this book: it describes the subject well enough, but to a Venetian of the Republic it would have seemed strange if not incomprehensible. Though the palaces included have been chosen according to architectural criteria, they owe their origin to a cross-section of the population. Seven were built for or were lived in by doges; three were built by *nouveaux riches* who purchased their place in the patriciate in the declining years of the Republic; two were built by humanists, and three for members of the citizen class. This last class represents a very distinct group; some of its members amassed great fortunes in trade, but most of them provided the Republic with her secretaries and chancery recorders. The ramification of the patrician family is represented by five palaces built for the Contarini family, four for the Loredan family, three each for the Pesaro and Mocenigo, and two each for six other families.

Characteristics of the Venetian Palace

The peculiar geographical situation of Venice in many ways determined the type of palace that was built there. And just as Venice is unique, so too the Venetian palace came to have characteristics not to be found elsewhere. Venice is made up of 117 islands, which cluster together in the centre of the lagoon. To the earliest inhabitants as well as to the refugees who came from the mainland later, this isolation meant safety and protection from their enemies. The earliest permanent houses built in the Middle Ages, like the still earlier wooden structures, did not need to be fortified like the houses of medieval Florence or Rome. And since Venice, unlike any other medieval Italian city, was remarkably free of internecine warfare, there seems to have been no need for the clan watch towers so familiar to students of the Florentine Guelphs and Ghibellines or Rome's feuding Colonna and Orsini. Why there were apparently no warring factions in medieval Venice remains something of a mystery and only now are scholars beginning to question it as a valid generalization. But observers of the Serenissima throughout her long history thought it was an historical fact and nothing short of a marvel. The Venetian propagandists boasted of it at every turn. Perhaps being so completely protected from invasion – and had not their situation saved them from the armies of the Holy Roman Emperor himself? – gave them a stronger sense of communal unity than existed in Florence or Rome, where treachery and betrayal of the city into the hands of a foreign power might mean the difference between political control and banishment or ruin for a clan or family. What fortification was necessary in Venice was provided by the state. The earliest palace of the doges was probably moated and fortified to protect the treasure of the Republic; and in the twelfth century the city undertook the considerable expense, given the technical difficulties, of erecting on piling and mud foundations the immense *campanile* as communal watch-tower, beacon, and bell-tower. Castellated defence towers also existed at different points in the city and from two of these an immense chain could effectively close the mouth of the Grand Canal to marauding ships expert enough to navigate that far through the shifting shoals and labyrinthine channels of the lagoon.

The openness of life within the city, still a characteristic of Venetian life today, is also illustrated by the fact that rich and poor lived, as Cassiodorus had observed, very much cheek by jowl. At no period did fashionable quarters develop like the Via Maggio in grand-ducal Florence or the Via Giulia in High Renaissance, papal Rome. A site on the Grand Canal had no particular

6. View across the Grand Canal showing (left to right) Palazzo Contarini dei Cavalli, Palazetto Tron and Palazzo Tron

7. OVERLEAF LEFT The Gothic Palazzo Barbaro

8. OVERLEAF RIGHT Baldassare Longhena's Palazzo Giustiniani-Lolin with part of the Gothic Palazzo Falier at San Vidal showing beyond

Introduction

social significance and many great families chose to build on the smaller side canals. Fine examples of Venetian domestic architecture do stand on the Grand Canal, but there are many equally important in other parts of the city.

The city, as every visitor knows, is divided into *sestieri*, or sixths, three on each side of the Grand Canal. In the days of the Republic, and to a great extent even today, it was the parish within the *sestiere* that determined one's 'quarter'. The parishes could be compared with the branches of the families within the aristocracy: in many ways they were equally autonomous. The branch of the family and the patriciate provided the two principal focuses for the individual patrician; the family unit was of lesser importance. And for all Venetians, the city as a whole, representing their patriotic duty to the state, and the parish, representing their daily life, were more important than the rather amorphous unit of the *sestiere*. The parish priests were elected by the parochial residents, the galley oarsmen and militia were chosen from parish lists, and many local people were employed by the nobles of the parish. The great families of the Republic were intimately identified with their parishes. The small houses around their *casa domenicale* or palace housed their dependants and retainers. The working people of the parish were godfathers to patrician children and noblemen stood sponsor for the children of the poor. The tutor engaged by the patrician for his young sons included their humbler playmates in his classes. But no single family branch or its palace dominated a parish. And yet no Venetian palace, whether on the Grand Canal or not, can be understood without examining its relationship to the squares, canals, quays, and churches of its parish.

The Venetian palace has certain characteristics which distinguish it from palaces built for the nobility in other Italian cities at similar periods. These characteristics are constant from the earliest surviving palaces down to the projects for palaces never built owing to the collapse of the Republic and the consequent bankruptcy of the family. All Venetian palaces have both a land and a water entrance. In the few instances where there seems to be no water entrance, this is usually due to the canal the palace overlooked having been filled in, often for health reasons, during the Austrian occupation. In some few cases, too, the water entrance did not give directly on the canal, but instead opened onto a *fondamenta*, or quay. The water-entrance side was always considered the principal façade, whether it gave onto the broad expanse of the Grand Canal, or a *fondamenta*, or even the darkest, humblest back canal or *rio*. It was this façade that in the earliest palaces displayed the owner's collection of Byzantine paterae, crosses and roundels, or plaques of precious marbles, and in the later palaces provided scope for an architect's individual fantasy and invention. No matter how much foreign architects of a later generation tried to stamp a façade with their own personality and idiom, certain elements to be found in the oldest houses remained constant.

The most striking feature of the Venetian palace façade is the central bank of windows on the first floor or *piano nobile*. This group of from three to six or more windows lit the long central hall, which ran the depth of the palace. In

9. The elaborately carved Istrian stone of the *piano nobile* at Palazzo Belloni

10. Lombardesque heraldic trophies and aedicular windows at Palazzo Contarini delle Figure, and right, late Gothic windows, balconies and details at Palazzo Erizzo

proportion something like a gallery, this central hall, or *portego*, ended in a similar group of windows which provided light from the land side. The windows to light the rooms on either side of the *portego* conformed to a certain pattern on the water and land façades. They were generally at least two in number on either side of the *portego* windows and were separated from one another by an expanse of wall, into which were built the fireplaces used to heat the side living-rooms. The windows on the lateral walls were generally placed at random, if indeed there were any at all. The only windows on the lateral walls that indicated what was behind them were the pairs of arched windows rising up the side to light the landings of the staircase, but these windows only became common in later centuries, when the staircase was incorporated into the fabric of the house.

The other feature common and constant in Venetian domestic architecture was the balconies, known in Venetian as *pergoli*. They appeared at an early date and were considered curious enough to be commented upon by visitors to the city; they never became so common a feature in Roman or Florentine domestic architecture. Since the Venetian palace façade is always more or less a flat rectangle without projecting wings to enliven the shape and without deep, shaded loggias or colonnades to relieve the flatness, it is the windows and balconies that provide most of the architectural interest.

Other features of the Venetian palace were determined not so much by conservative local traditions as by the restricted area available. Obviously, a group of small mud-flat islands would make it impossible for even the richest patrician to have more than limited land for his house. As a result, palaces were very often not only built right next to one another, but frequently used the earlier walls of an adjoining house as part of the newer construction. This was why the Venetian palace with exposed lateral walls rarely displayed carefully designed windows; neither were the lateral walls decorated.

The Venetian palace was, until the seventeenth century and after, a solid block. It did not enclose a *cortile* in the manner of the Florentine palace. The courtyard or garden area stood behind the house and was created, in the Gothic period at least, by simply enclosing a space with a high brick wall. One or two sides of the courtyard might contain rooms, and later a third wing might be built around the courtyard to enlarge the palace. The façades, and especially the water façade with its projecting balconies, remained the principal focus of the house and a *cortile* with inward-facing loggias never became a part of the native architectural repertoire. The restricted building site also meant there was little space for a monumental staircase such as became common in the houses of Florence and Rome.

Venetian Palace Construction

The construction of a Venetian palace and the building materials employed remained the same throughout the long history of the Republic's surviving buildings. The most significant variations occurred in the sixteenth and later

centuries, but they were, for the most part, confined to detail or decoration; the basic structure and even the plan was remarkably untouched by innovation. When the elementary foundation of a house was that of the hard island clay, no piling or shoring was needed. Such instances are very rare, given the need to reinforce any sort of ground for larger buildings and also given the scarcity of such solid ground. For the most part, the Venetian palace rests on a composite foundation of piling and filler. The wood used for the piling was oak that had been cut into two-metre lengths with a diameter of 20 to 25 cm., and had then been left to soak in brackish water. The oak came originally from nearby groves on the lido and the mainland, but later builders preferred wood from Dalmatia. To drive the piles below the low-tide level, a coffer-dam arrangement was built on the site. Planking marked off the site and was shored up and sealed with a clay embankment. The inside of this precinct was then dug and baled out, and the piles were driven in by two men wielding a heavy two-handled weight. In later centuries, when longer piling came into use, the pile-drivers hauled a heavier weight up a tall shaft with a system of ropes and pulleys and then freed it to drop on the head of the pile from the top of the shaft. This is the system still used in Venice today; only the rhythmic chants of the pile-drivers have disappeared. Where modern engineers have examined the pilings, an interesting development has emerged. Under the oldest buildings, such as the Basilica and the *campanile*, the pilings are generally short and widely spaced. Under more recent buildings, like the seventeenth-century basilica of the Salute, the piles are considerably longer than the two-metre average and are very tightly packed together. The earlier raft principle floated great loads whereas later builders wanted their buildings firmly anchored in the harder subsoil of the lagoon. In the case of the palaces, pilings were only laid along the perimeter of the site and beneath the major sustaining walls. When the piling was sunk, it was levelled and packed with clay. A specially hard clay was used for this and other sealing operations, and the Venetian government imposed heavy fines on those who removed clay from the pits without a licence.

After the piling had been levelled and packed, 2.5 cm.-thick planking of larch, walnut or, later, mahogany was laid criss-cross to cover the foundation area. On this planking the wall base was laid in brick, still well below the high-tide level. The bricks used at this stage, and indeed throughout the wall construction, were either the thin, flat type used in the oldest buildings and copied from the brick of the Romans (40–50 cm. × 25 cm. × 5 cm.) or else an even thinner brick, only 3 cm. thick, known as the *communella*. By the fifteenth century deep-red Venetian brick was used almost universally. Its dimensions (26 cm. × 13 cm. × 6 cm.) are similar to the modern brick and it is still used in the city's buildings today.

At the ground level of the walls a course of Istrian stone was laid. The *pietra d'Istria* served to tie the masonry together, provided a solid base for the tall walls that would rise above, and owing to its density, was a protection against rising damp. The external walls of the lower floors were, on the average, three

11. The Veneto-Byzantine style water-gate arcade at Ca' d'Oro

Introduction

to four Venetian bricks thick; the upper floors' outside walls were only two bricks thick to reduce the weight load. The mortar used was kneaded sand and lime. Raw limestone was used in early times, but later on burnt limestone became common. In the oldest buildings that survive in Venice, only the external brick course was cemented, while the inner course was often simply dry-wall construction. As for finishing the walls, the masons sealed or pointed the brickwork, but from an early date external walls were also plastered. A stucco of pulverized brick was mixed with a solution of lime and applied over the brickwork, the joints of which were scored with a nail to ensure adherence. Antique *intonaco*, or plaster, was a mixture of pulverized brick and grains of marble, whereas modern *intonaco* is made of synthetic paints and sand. The internal walls were of the same thickness as the master walls; but partitions added at later dates are sometimes as much as 30 cm. thick to provide a suitable thickness for heavy stone door-frames. These partition walls were constructed of light, rough boarding and were either rubble-filled or hollow, and their external surface was covered with lathing to secure the stucco finishing. It cannot be often enough emphasized how constant these elements of Venetian palace construction remained throughout the centuries.

Even more remarkable is the fact that the basic plan of the Venetian palace remained unaltered for so long, even though exceptions and minor variations were introduced according to the fashions and architectural innovations of a given period. Most palaces are symmetrical: the main hall, called *sala del portego*, is in the centre, with an equal number of rooms on either side of it. However, in some of the most important palaces, the central hall ends in an L or a T on the canal front, making the façade asymmetric and affecting the disposition of the side rooms. But even such an apparently significant deviation from the norm does not invalidate the archetype: the L and T branches of the *portego* are simply side rooms opened into it to enlarge its space.

The central element of the ground-floor plan of all Venetian palaces is the *andron*, the hall behind the water-gate entrance. The *andron* runs the depth of the palace, and in houses where there is a mezzanine, it is higher than the other ground-floor rooms because it includes the height of the mezzanine floor as well. The *andron* was the principal entrance hall, though given the double function of the early Venetian palace (as both place of business and residence of the patrician merchant) it served commercial as well as ceremonial purposes. Some misconceptions have grown up around its use and are frequently repeated. For instance, it is said to have been the space where the gondolas were stored; but in fact, in the days of the Republic gondolas were always in the water, unless they were being painted or repaired. Occasional repairs may have been done in the *andron* if the owner did not patronize one of the city's innumerable boatyards. Lighters from the Republic's merchant fleet were unloaded into the *andron*, though it is doubtful that such a dark and generally damp and draughty area would have been used for either display or storage of stuffs and spices as has often been claimed.

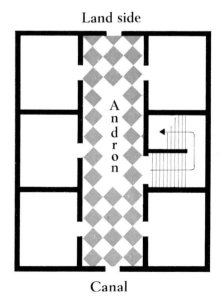

Land side

A n d r o n

Canal

12. Simplified ground floor plan of a Venetian palace with internal staircase

26

The rooms on either side of the *andron* were the store-rooms both in the period when the house was an emporium of the *casa fondaco* type and later, too, when the house was exclusively a patrician residence. The number of these rooms varied with the depth of the building, though three on each side of the *andron* was common in the period when the internal staircase was built in the space of the middle room on one side. It was also in these dark ground-floor rooms that the kitchens were located, and huge hooded cooking fireplaces and stone water-troughs can still be found in some of them.

The *andron* was the only ground-floor room which was treated in much the same way in all houses. Its length was paved with alternating, diagonally laid squares of white Istrian stone and a red-veined marble from Cattaro in Dalmatia, and its brick walls were covered with dark-stained boarding to protect them from damp. Simple stone or wooden benches were attached to the walls, and in later centuries were provided with tall wooden backs fitted flush to the wall, elaborately carved in outline, and painted with coats of arms to record a matrimonial alliance. Such armorial pride was by then a hollow echo of the earlier period, when the *andron* was lined with a display of suits of the finest Milanese and German armour: swords, poniards, pikes, and halberds were arranged in trophies with the captured prizes and banners of enemy navies. The *andron* was frequently lit by torches housed in the immense stern lantern of a captain's galley or in the giant three-branched *fanale* from an admiral's flagship. Later a hanging lantern became the more usual lighting fixture, many examples from the seventeenth and eighteenth centuries being elaborate confections of wrought-iron foliage and cartouches. The storage rooms needed no decoration, but even so the heavy iron bars of their simple windows were soon treated to considerable elaboration. From a projecting, cage-like grill, they were later mounted flush in the window-frame with the bars threaded diagonally through one another; later still, the iron was worked in complicated rosette patterns or else was made of vertical bars bombéed to echo a popular type of eighteenth-century wrought-iron balcony.

One of the most significant structural modifications to the Venetian palace took place when the external staircase at the back of the house was replaced by one inside the building itself. Generally speaking, this innovation dates from the late fifteenth or early sixteenth century. But as long as Gothic-style palaces were built in Venice, the external staircase was an integral part. It rose in two flights at right angles to one another and was supported on stone-moulded lancet arches made of brick and gradated with the rise of the stairs. Plain stone columnettes without bases supported a flat stair-rail, except at the landings, where the columnettes were joined to the rail with tiny inflected pointed arches. The rail itself was sometimes decorated with carved human heads or lions *sejant*. The uppermost landing was often covered by a small roof built on beams projecting from the wall and supported by two columns rising from the balustrade. The porch thus made was called a *liagò* and later gave its name to the completely enclosed balcony rooms popular in the eighteenth century. The external staircase of the Venetian Gothic house rose to the *piano*

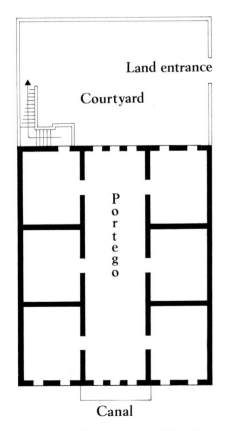

13. Plan of the *piano nobile* of a Venetian palace with a Gothic external staircase

Introduction

nobile, but in the double-plan or two-family house, a second external staircase rose along the walls of a separate courtyard to the living quarters on the floor above, the second *piano nobile*.

In the early fifteenth century, an intermediate floor between the ground floor and the *piano nobile* was introduced, and it remained a distinctive feature of Venetian palace architecture and living ever after. The *mezzà*, or mezzanine, was made out of the upper section of the storage rooms on either side of the *andron* and contained therefore two separate sets of rooms. Early on the two were linked by a passageway across the *andron* near the water entrance. As an integral part of the storage rooms, the mezzanines originally served as business offices where records, accounts, and archives were housed. When the commercial function of the house began to diminish, and its aristocratic pretensions became more prominent, collections of rare books, manuscripts, gems, and scientific instruments were added to the family archives, and the mezzanine gradually became the library and repository of the family's varied treasures. Only in the seventeenth and eighteenth centuries, when the principal rooms of the *piano nobile* became vast, were the cosier and more easily heated rooms of the mezzanine used as sitting-rooms and bedrooms.

The earliest mezzanine apartments, separate from one another on either side of the *andron*, had on the one side a secondary staircase leading up from the ground floor. When the principal staircase was built inside the house, its landing gave access to the other mezzanine. The staircase joined the *portego* through an archway, which was often highly decorated in the Renaissance and in later centuries. Broken or interrupted pediments, lolling tutelary gods and goddesses, cavorting cupids, trophies and helmets, and occasional Latin mottoes adorned the staircase arches in a profusion found nowhere else in the house. Even so the typical Venetian staircase was not as grand as its Roman or Florentine counterpart. Narrow and steep, it rose in two flights interrupted by a single landing lit by two generous round-arched windows. The treads and mouldings were of *pietra d'Istria* and the landing might be paved with a pattern of polished variegated marble or a design worked in *terrazzo*. There was no room on such narrow flights for elaborate stone balustrades, so heavy silk-covered ropes hanging in heavy loops between brass lion's-head mounts became the traditional Venetian stair-rails.

But the most significant feature of the internal staircase was the vaulting. Though it was only a simple barrel-vault, with perhaps an uncomplicated cross-vault over the landing, it is none the less interesting, for this type of construction had no place at all elsewhere in Venetian domestic architecture. There were no cellars where vaults might have provided reinforcement, and the walls, being of brick, were not subject to the stresses that vaulting relieved in stone structures. Naturally enough, vaulting was used in the relieving arches of windows and occasionally in doorways, but a vaulted ceiling in a Venetian palace would be a contradiction in terms. The coved and frescoed ceilings of the eighteenth century were all 'false' and had nothing to do with

14. The seventeenth-century staircase arch in the *portego* of Palazzo Giustinian-Recanati

the structure of the building. Vaulting was, however, used elsewhere in the city's architecture. Most prominently, it appeared in all sorts of combinations in the churches and, less noticeably, in the many rain-water cisterns under the raised *campi*.

From the *andron*, up the principal stairway, one arrives directly in the *portego*, the central hall; there are no antechambers, corridors, or galleries to pass through. In fact, the *sala del portego* of the *piano nobile* might be conveniently, if inaccurately, described as a gallery. Its Venetian dialect name recalls the word *portico* and indicates that the group of tall windows providing light from either end were, in the earlier palaces, unglazed. The *portego* hall running the depth of the house in its centre was, like the identically proportioned *andron* below, really a passageway, a grandiose corridor open at either end – in short, a gallery *cum* portico. Its function as a gallery explains much of its traditional furnishing: there were no fireplaces, and *portego* furniture was designed to stand impressively along the walls with no consideration for comfort. The variation in plan of the Venetian *portego* has already been alluded to: generally it was a straight, narrow hall in the centre, but in some houses the end overlooking the water terminated in T or L branches, and in an asymmetrical palace the *portego* had rooms along one side of it only. In any case, it was the principal hall of the house.

Typical of the Venetian *portego*, as well as of the rest of the house, was its flooring. There is evidence that the *portego* was paved with brick in the earliest period when it was open to the elements. Board flooring may also have been used in the older houses, but soon *terrazzo* flooring became traditional for all the rooms of a Venetian palace. A layer of this type has been uncovered in the Ca' d'Oro and may well be contemporary with the early fifteenth-century construction of the building. On top of a base of planks, a cement-like paste made of ground rubble and lime was laid, and then a third layer, which would be polished and would serve as the floor. Its ingredients depended on the taste of the owner, but generally included bits of white burnt limestone, and coloured marble laid in a crushed brick and lime paste giving the floors their typical red-brown hue. The more elaborate *terrazzo* floors also included nuggets of glass, mother of pearl, or the golden tesserae used in mosaic work. The various chunks and bits of stone were cut or planed to an approximately smooth surface, over which a linseed-oil and plaster filler was poured. The whole was then levelled and polished with ever finer abrasive stones. *Terrazzo* was a very light material, weight always being a prime consideration in building on Venetian foundations. It also had the virtue of elasticity, so that when the building settled unevenly, as was inevitably the case, the floor stretched more and cracked less than a floor laid in marble or terracotta tile squares. When a crack did appear or a fault caused a section of the *terrazzo* to crumble, spot repairs were simple. If shifting did much damage, a new surface could be laid over the old without putting too much weight on the supporting beams.

The laying and re-laying of *terrazzo* in layers explains the rather boring

15. The mezzanine and elegant water-gate of Palazzo Gussoni

sameness of the floors in Venetian palaces. Most of the surviving *terrazzo* floors in Venice were laid in the nineteenth century or in the early years of this century. But a few floors laid in the days of the Republic do survive. They are very rich, colourful, and often elaborate. A twisted-ribbon border or delicate garlands of simple flowers were not uncommon patterns worked in the coloured stones of a Venetian *terrazzo*; in the *portego*, an elaborately framed coat of arms was frequently the central motif.

While no decorated *terrazzo* floors laid before the seventeenth century survive in Venetian palaces, various documents and paintings describe some of the decoration of the walls of the *portego* and living-rooms in earlier periods. Before and during the sixteenth century, stamped and gilded leather lined the rooms from the floor to a height of two or three metres. At that height a shelf-like cornice framed the leather and provided a place for the display of bronzes, rare glass, vases, plate, and other *objets d'art*. The use of stamped leather seems at first a taste influenced by Spanish fashion, but from the fifteenth century there was a state-supervised manufactory for working and decorating leather that came to Venice from Tana on the Black Sea. Tapestry hangings would have been more common in Venice at the same period had the government supported its manufacture locally as was done at Florence and Ferrara. Instead the Venetian weaver worked more with raw material of the Levantine trade and consequently the walls of the *portego* and other rooms were early hung with silks, brocades, and damask. In the later seventeenth century, an influx of skilled stuccadors from near Lugano gave rise to the highly elaborate decorative work still characteristic of the richest *portego* decoration. Enormous mythological oil paintings were bought and cut to fit the exuberantly decorated frames of the stuccoed hall. A reaction to this extravaganza of stucco-work was inevitable and with the arrival of a more sober, neoclassical taste, *marmorino* came to be used to decorate the *portego* walls. *Marmorino* is marble dust mixed and applied like paint. With varying hues of marble, the appearance of veined marble slabs could be created by the painter, and when the surface had been finished by polishing, it cleverly counterfeited the glowing, rich effect of real marble. The skill and time used by the worker in *marmorino* might easily cost his employer more than real marble would have done; hence even this less elaborate fashion still appealed to the patrician taste for extravagance. Even had he wanted real marble slabs to decorate his walls, it is doubtful that the architect would have allowed it. Weight was always an essential factor, even in the decoration of the interior of a Venetian palace.

The only place where heavy materials were used inside a house was in the door and window frames. These were generally of Istrian stone, but only in the case of the staircase arch were they ever heavily decorated. After the seventeenth century, red Verona marble was often used for the door frames and at about the same time the columns of the staircase arch began to be quarried from rare, veined and variegated marbles.

The lighting of the *sala del portego* also followed conventions that were modified only according to the fashions of the day. Brass chandeliers of the type seen in Flemish painting were hung in the late Gothic period, then lanterns of the type that remained traditional for the *andron* were introduced. Before the manufacture of sheet glass was perfected, these lanterns were glazed with thin glass rods. The curvature and thickness of the rods made them no more transparent than the roundels used in the windows at about this time, but at least both were translucent. In the late seventeenth century, the elaborately contrived and coloured chandeliers of Murano glass became fashionable. Jointed to produce a tangle of rococo curves, and dotted about with miniature glass pots holding detachable coloured glass flowers, these delicate contraptions could be dismantled for shipment and reassembled in the palace. This practical construction allowed for the widespread exportation of Venetian taste in chandeliers to Rococo palaces everywhere in Europe. Murano looking-glasses and mirror-backed sconces were also sold throughout Europe and were, of course, to be found in abundance in Venetian palaces decorated in the eighteenth century.

The furniture of the *portego* was, as has been mentioned, designed more for show than comfort. This distinction could hardly be made in the earlier periods, when most furniture was on a monumental scale by modern standards. But by the eighteenth century, when the comfortably upholstered settee or armchair became common, the furniture designed for the Venetian *portego* was easy to distinguish. The most common piece was an exceptionally long settee with a seat covered in silk. Its back was uncomfortably vertical because it was meant to stand against the *portego* wall, and in design it was virtually a trellis-work carved in the ribbon fancies of eighteenth-century taste. Tiny little tripod tables called *trespoli* and the *guéridons*, or decorative blackamoors, both of minimal functional value, completed the sparse furnishing of an area that remained, until the fall of the Republic, basically a gallery or glorified corridor. In the nineteenth century, the impractical *portego* was often partitioned off into cosier and more manageable sections or else a grand staircase was built at the back to rise through a section of its vastness. Both transformations cut down the daylight, which had always been considered an essential element of Venetian palace living and design.

The concern with light in houses that could often only have windows on the front and rear walls can be illustrated by a detail of interior decoration that is respected even today: the Venetian window is generally covered only by white gauze curtains, gathered and ruched into scallop folds and raised vertically. These curtains admitted a maximum amount of light while cutting the water-reflected glare. Above eighteenth-century windows, there were carved and gilded pelmets hung with rich brocades and velvets, and panels of the same materials often hung on either side of the window as well. But these panels were never full-sized curtains meant to be drawn across the windows themselves. This particular fashion was also copied throughout the world, even in climates where the original practical considerations were meaningless.

What has been described above is for the most part typical of that most

Introduction

characteristic feature of the Venetian palace, the *sala del portego*. But the floor, window, and wall decoration was substantially the same in the rooms on either side of the central hall, save that some types of decoration, such as elaborate stucco-work, were particularly suited to the size and formality of the *portego*. The essential difference between the *portego* and the side rooms was in their function. The side rooms were the living-rooms of the palace: the sitting-rooms, bedrooms, and the room where the family ate. It is easy to forget that for a long time the latter might be any of the rooms and only late in the eighteenth century, if then, was a specific room set aside for eating. Furniture was then, as the Italians still call it, *mobile*: movable. Life in a Venetian palace of the Republic cannot be imagined unless today's visitor can conjure up the numerous retainers who shifted and carried the furniture around to suit their masters' taste or else loaded the better part onto barges and then ox-drawn carts for the seasonal migration to the villas of the mainland.

Like the extensive use of comfortably upholstered furniture and the warm carpets of the Orient that covered the floors and tables, the installation of fireplaces in the side rooms indicates the importance attached to comfort and livability. The earliest fireplaces may have been the huge hooded hearths commonly found in Tuscany today and surviving in some of the old Venetian palace kitchens. By the sixteenth century, the hood projected less into the room and a prominent mantelpiece supported by handsome stone caryatids was commissioned from a sculptor. Examples by Sansovino and Alessandro Vittoria still survive in private houses. In the eighteenth century, the hoods disappeared into the wall, leaving a flat surface above the mantel for the elaborately framed and costly looking-glasses of Murano. The fireplace itself was reduced to a simple marble frame around the hearth as a foil to the exuberant looking-glass frame. At this date, and even earlier, the fireplace was backed with Venetian ceramic tiles, which are often mistaken for Delft tiles because of the fine workmanship and the predominance of blue and white in their designs. Under the Austrian occupation, many fireplaces were blocked up to make way for the *Kachelöfen* or Austrian ceramic tile stoves. Several fine examples of this heating apparatus exist today, but many were destroyed in the burst of anti-Austrian sentiment which followed the Unification of Italy, and others disappeared more prosaically with the arrival of central heating. As a result, many side rooms in Venetian palaces are today without trace of stove or fireplace, yet even a casual examination of the lateral walls indicates how numerous the fireplaces must have been.

One last remark might be made about Venetian furnishing. When the fashion for monumental oak furniture – prevalent everywhere in Europe – began to wane, the Venetians made little use of the delicate veneers, *intarsia*, and marquetry work popular elsewhere, but preferred lacquer for the important furniture of their houses. This was undoubtedly due to their contacts with the Orient, but the damp climate of the city must have been a consideration, too. The one place where the Venetians did use veneer work extensively was in the doors of the house. These are most often of a walnut veneer cut across the grain in large panels and held in place by a heavy moulding frame stained a darker colour. A similar moulding is repeated in rectangles and squares in the centre of the doors, giving them a solid and monumental appearance. Delicate lacquer doors did sometimes replace these sombre older doors and a particularly fine one from a series with chinoiserie designs attributed to Tiepolo still exists.

The ceiling construction of a Venetian house was partly determined by available materials and, more significantly, by the need to keep all structural components as light as possible. The basic Venetian ceiling consists of beams, which were cut from larch or fir trees around Cadore and brought down the Piave river in rafts. The span of the beams varied with the width of the room; their section was generally 20 by 25 cm. and they were laid one to two widths apart. Coniferous timber was not only light, but its natural resins were protection against the damp of the lagoon climate. One or two layers of boarding were laid on the beams to provide the base for the *terrazzo* flooring above. Battens were fixed on the joints of the beams and boarding, giving the earliest ceilings a shallow coffered pattern. The battens and beams of the *piano nobile* were often decorated with simple painted designs in the Gothic period. The ceiling 'alla Sansovino', which antedated the arrival of that architect in Venice, was of the same construction though more elaborately decorated: the beams were completely painted and their edges and designs were often picked out in gilt. Classical brackets, painted and gilded, were inserted between the beams along the walls and a carved frieze ran beneath. In the sixteenth century false ceilings became predominant. The earliest consisted of heavy and elaborately carved gilded frames set with oil paintings on canvas. In the seventeenth and eighteenth centuries, a network of light lattice work was suspended from the beams by long iron rods and then covered with reeds tied with twine. The whole was plastered over to provide a base for fresco decoration. The flexibility of the reed and twine structure allowed for curvature, coving, and even the impression of vaulting. At the same time the stuccadors often used a combination of the two false ceilings: the earlier frame ceiling was the basic unit, with three-dimensional stucco fantasies often realized over reed and twine armatures. The most elaborate ceiling decoration was obviously reserved for the principal rooms of the *piano nobile*. The ceilings of the other floors were simply of painted beams or, where there was a flat false ceiling, were decorated with the palette-knife ribbons and cartouches of the stuccador.

The floors above the *piano nobile* were reached by secondary staircases. In the Gothic house, which had a single external staircase leading only to the principal floor, a steep single flight of internal stairs built of wood, with lattice-work balustrades, led to the upper floors. In later houses, the secondary staircase might be barrel-vaulted like the principal one or perhaps of the spiral type popular in the sixteenth century. The plan of the second *piano nobile* repeated that of the main floor, complete with *portego* and side rooms. The use of these rooms is somewhat difficult to determine, but it is most probable that

Introduction

they provided the sleeping quarters for the children of the family and for lesser relations. Servants lived in the attics above or were housed in the small buildings owned by the family in the neighbourhood.

The roof of the palace was constructed like that of any hipped-roof building and was covered with locally fired cylindrical-section terracotta tiles. Its only specifically Venetian characteristic was the king-post suspended above the tie-beam and fastened to it by iron brackets. The space between the tie-beam and the king-post gives the flexibility required in a building that might be expected to shift and settle on its foundations.

The joinery work in a Venetian palace occasionally reveals the hand of carpenters trained in a boatyard, for instance in the case of the *altana* or traditional roof-top platform. Reached by ladder or even by a proper small staircase, the *altana* was a terrace on which linen could be dried or carpets aired. Visitors to Venice also noted that the ladies of the house resorted to the *altana* to bleach their hair in the sun. Besides the *altana*, an integral part of the Venetian roofscape was the chimneys, which likewise have a distinctive identity. The most common terminated in an up-ended cone, which served as a spark-trap – a necessary precaution in a town where the chimneys were numerous and the houses were built very close together. Though its function as a spark-trap remained constant, the chimney assumed many different shapes. The design of this last traditional detail of the palace was not left to chance. It was the specific responsibility, and part of the training, of the apprentice architect working on a house to design an original, but functional chimney with which to top off the building.

16. Chimneys of Palazzo Dario

The Development of Palace Architecture

As has been stated above, the building materials and the general plan remained remarkably constant in the tradition of Venetian palace building, in a way they did nowhere else. Though travertine, *macigno* and *pietra serena* were frequently used in the construction of Roman and Florentine palaces and the plan of a building enclosing a loggia or arcaded courtyard could be said to provide an archetype for both cities, there are too many important exceptions to the rule in both plan and elevation to speak conveniently or accurately of a Roman or a Florentine palace type. In Venice, certain generalizations hold true and the fashions of succeeding periods only slightly modified the outward appearance or interior layout of the palaces. Stylistic innovation seems to have been approached with caution by the Venetian patrician and accepted with reluctance.

In other cities in Italy, the stylistic characteristics of a palace may well be an important clue to when it was built and by whom. The issue is more complicated in Venice. The peculiar mixture of eclecticism and conservatism makes it extremely difficult to discuss the dating or origins of a Venetian palace unless documentary evidence substantiates one's guess. For example, scholars have differed by as much as four hundred years when attempting to date the earliest surviving Venetian palace, even when they do manage to agree on which particular building deserves the honour. And when it comes to determining the prototype of these early buildings, no solution yet offered has met with general acceptance. Of the most discussed candidates as prototype, two seem most likely and are therefore bones of the most violent contention. Unfortunately, not enough remains of the right type of imperial Roman villa or palace – or perhaps a hybrid combination of the two – to qualify convincingly. By the same token, nothing of the right date survives within the boundaries of the Byzantine empire to prove that the Venetians might have taken their model from the East. It is most likely that elements of both were combined into what became the earliest buildings in Venice recognizable as palaces. Without examining all the generally inconclusive arguments of architectural historians, it may be said that elements of Diocletian's fourth-century villa-palace at Spalato (today's Split) could easily have influenced Venetian builders. This monument was, and is even today, impressive enough and was certainly known to the earliest Venetian merchants whose ships plied the coast of Dalmatia. The seaside site of the palace made it eminently suitable for adaptation to Venetian conditions and the fact that it is remarkably little fortified for a building of its size and importance could make it a model of that characteristic of the early Venetian palace. The architectural feature echoed in the earliest Venetian palaces is the long seaside arcade of Diocletian's building, flanked as it is by two towers. No other building of sufficient antiquity incorporates this particular feature.

From the East, and most probably from Byzantine Constantinople itself, the Venetian architect copied and incorporated details of decoration. The arches of the early Venetian palace arcade were not of imperial Roman design, but were similar to the stilted arches of Byzantium. The carved arabesque motifs of the basket capitals and the use of decorative paterae and marble plaques were deeply influenced by Constantinople. The arches and decorative details give a distinctly oriental air to those early buildings and consequently they have been described by most architectural historians as Veneto-Byzantine palaces. The earliest to survive are probably of the thirteenth century, though recent investigations have shown that some of these incorporate features and details of eleventh-century buildings.

The archetypal Veneto-Byzantine palace was two storeys tall with an arcade called a *curia*, which extended the width of the façade on both the ground and first floors and was flanked by two slightly taller towers. The only palace left in Venice which gives an approximate idea (and that as a result of radical nineteenth-century restoration and reconstruction) of this scheme is the Fondaco dei Turchi. The arcaded Byzantine palace might seem at first glance to have little or no relation to the traditional palace type described earlier. But if one pictures the first-floor arcading reduced to the openings which lit the later *portego*, and the flanking towers or *torreselle* enlarged to incorporate the side rooms, the traditional tripartite façade of the Venetian palace can be seen to have evolved from these early buildings. One feature of

Introduction

the Byzantine palace that completely disappeared in time was the *riva*, the shore in front of the house. Early maps and views of the city show that the first palaces were not built on the water's edge, but like the seaside façade of Diocletian's palace, they were set back from the water. The narrow stretch of shore in front of the Byzantine palace allowed the merchant's lighters to be beached for unloading or repair.

The nineteenth-century reconstruction, debatable as it is, of the Fondaco dei Turchi (the emporium of the Turkish merchants) gives us an idea of some of the features of the Veneto-Byzantine palace that remained characteristic of that phase of Venetian palace construction. Projecting balconies did not appear until the fifteenth century, possibly earlier; instead, balustrades were inserted flush between the columns of the arcades. In many cases there were not proper balustrades, but rather *plutei* carved with various Byzantine geometric patterns or stylized figurative motifs. The *plutei* are a borrowing from ecclesiastical décor and indeed the entire arch group of the Veneto-Byzantine palace could have had as its prototype the stilted-arch porch arcade of a building like the eleventh-century church of Santa Fosca at Torcello. Without straining to establish a documented link between the two, it is sufficient to note the extent to which ecclesiastical motifs were present in the decoration of twelfth- and thirteenth-century Veneto-Byzantine palaces: *plutei*, basket capitals with crosses interwoven in the patterned carving, stilted arches, *paterae*, and carved plaques. Both the *paterae* and the *plutei* could have been carved by local stonecutters, but it is just as likely that many were taken as booty, relics, or perhaps as good-luck tokens from an actual church. After the conquest of Constantinople in 1204, the Venetian republic required its merchants to bring back in their ships a certain percentage of the value of their cargo in works of art for the embellishment of the city. Much of the Byzantine stone carving in the city may have come from Constantinople, serving as ballast on the voyage and displayed on arrival as trophies of conquest. A fine collection of *paterae* is still to be seen on the façade of the Palazzo da Mosto, which also has two marble plaques at the corners carved to represent blind arches – a motif frequently found embedded in the remains of other Veneto-Byzantine façades and probably derived in design from the blind arches used in the decoration of early Venetian church apses, façades, and bell-towers.

The Fondaco dei Turchi, the Palazzo da Mosto, and the Palazzo Loredan all illustrate the use of marble facing on the Veneto-Byzantine façade. The Fondaco also provides a reconstruction, from old maps and plans, of the castellated parapet made of marble plaques surmounted by stone spheres. All traces of these parapets have disappeared in the surviving Veneto-Byzantine palaces because upper floors have been superimposed on their original two-storey height. Only the later Gothic parapets of the ducal palace and the Ca' d'Oro testify now to the popularity of this decorative trim. The Loredan, da Mosto, and Donà della Madonnetta palaces all illustrate the use of dentil moulding to outline the arch faces.

17. Byzantine capitals, concave group (John Ruskin, *The Stones of Venice* 1851–53)

36

The shape of the arches permits a provisional chronology of Veneto-Byzantine construction when there is no precise way of dating these buildings. Ruskin's chart of Venetian arch types remains the most widely respected. It is based on the idea that the simplest arches came first and were subject to elaboration at a later date. Thus the simple stilted arches of the Fondaco, the Loredan and Donà houses appear to be of the oldest type; the keystones at the Palazzo da Mosto and the Palazzo Falier indicate a later date; and the arches of the Priuli-Bon house at San Stae illustrate a third stage of development and hint at the transition to the Gothic arch. The most interesting of these palaces is probably the Palazzo da Mosto, not only for the richness and authenticity of its decoration, nor merely for the air of genuine antiquity due to its dilapidated condition, but because it illustrates so many of the problems facing the architectural historian trying to date, describe, and reconstruct a Veneto-Byzantine house.

To begin with, an arch of the *piano nobile* and an arch of the ground floor have been blocked, thus destroying the symmetry of the façade. The original volume of the building has been disguised by the addition of floors above the *piano nobile*, and of course, any tower-like elevations, *torreselle*, or parapets, that may have existed have disappeared altogether as a result. Recent study has shown that dating the building is extremely complicated. The carving of the ground-floor arch has been ascribed to the eleventh and twelfth centuries while the arches of the *piano nobile* are demonstrably, and in agreement with Ruskin's system, of the twelfth and thirteenth centuries. The capitals of the *piano nobile* columns were probably remade in the fourteenth century. Thus, even in the smallest details, the Palazzo da Mosto is a good example of the eclecticism that was to be typical of Venetian building for centuries to come. The better part of the palace is twelfth to thirteenth century to be sure, but incorporates important elements of an earlier building, probably destroyed in the fire that swept the Rialto area in the twelfth century. Then there are the significant modifications of later centuries as well.

The da Mosto house is located near the Rialto, the ancient market, exchange, and banking centre of the earliest settlement in Venice. Almost all the surviving Veneto-Byzantine houses are to be found nearby: the palaces known as the Loredan, Farsetti, Barzizza, Businello, Donà and Falier. The da Mosto and Falier palaces taken together represent the survival of a real unit of the early Veneto-Byzantine settlement near the Rialto. They were built adjacent and almost interlocking in function on the same island: the former faces the Grand Canal, while the latter gives onto a small rio. The Palazzo Falier is built out over its *fondamenta*, thus creating one of the oldest *sottoporteghi* in the city. This was a passage under a building or, as its Venetian name makes clear, under the *portego* or main hall of a house. This co-existence of public passageway and private property is easy to misinterpret. The *calli* or small streets of Venice were in fact owned by the proprietors of the buildings that lined them. The *sottoportego* of the Palazzo Falier is an integral part of the building, and in this and other later palaces the role of the *sottoportego* must be

Introduction

kept in proper perspective. It represented a mixture of practical necessity and a sort of *noblesse oblige*, and should never be considered a mere decorative adjunct, no matter how much an architect might do to embellish its original function.

Two palaces represent particularly well the stylistic transition from Veneto-Byzantine to Gothic architecture in Venice. The first is the Priuli-Bon house (of the late thirteenth or early fourteenth century) near the Fondaco dei Turchi. It still has traces of a ground-floor arcade of Byzantine stilted arches while the *piano nobile* arches are of proto-Gothic cusped intrados and extrados, or double-inflected type. The second palace, the mid-fourteenth-century Palazzo Sagredo, not only illustrates the further stages of the transition to Gothic in its mezzanine windows, but is a palimpsest of later developments in Venetian Gothic as well.

Even where the arches of windows are obviously Gothic in form and detail, Venetian Gothic is quite different from what the northern visitor might expect. This was the difference that fascinated the young Ruskin, and in his indispensable analysis of Venetian building, *The Stones of Venice* (1851–3), he writes about what happened to the style, indigenous to the north, when it arrived in Venice. As Ruskin realized, the site was a determinant factor. Since stone buildings could not be well supported on Venice's mud and piling foundations, brick was used as the basic material. This meant that the elaborate stone carving typical of northern Gothic would be absent to a large degree in Venetian Gothic. As has been mentioned earlier, brick walls were not subject to the extreme stresses of stone walls, so neither vaults nor buttresses elaborated with tracery and statuary were needed or desired. The siting on the water's edge necessitated a flat façade that made the most of the restricted space available; the irregular plan of a Gothic house such as that of the merchant Jacques Coeur at Bourges, with bulky round towers and meandering wings, was not feasible. A planar style, derived in part from the Veneto-Byzantine palace, predominated and the varied volumes and shapes of northern Gothic remained foreign to Venice.

In the Gothic period, roughly the fourteenth and fifteenth centuries, the role of the architect begins to emerge. This is not to say that a Venetian Gothic palace is the work of an architect recognized as such, or even that one man might be responsible for its design. Venetian Gothic architecture was the result of a highly eccentric mixture of tradition and innovation, of the collaboration of patron and workmen, and of these workmen and their *capomastro* or construction foreman. More often than not it was the latter who was responsible for the building's distinctive features, and more often than not he was by training a stonecutter. Stone was used in Venice for decorative elements, and in the Gothic palace that meant tracery, moulding, arch shapes, capitals, balconies, friezes, finials and the like. From the records concerning the construction of later Gothic palaces, like the remarkably complete archive for the Ca' d'Oro, one can generalize to some extent about the sources of Venetian Gothic architecture and the influence brought to bear on its

18. Fifteenth-century Gothic corner cable-moulding, dentil-moulding frames and sixth-type Gothic windows with finials at Palazzo Pesaro degli Orfei

19. Gothic capitals (John Ruskin, *The Stones of Venice* 1851–53)

development by the stonecutters and their teams of workmen. First, as can be seen from the traditional divisions and symmetry of the façade, domestic architecture in Venice was to a great extent determined by local tradition. But the records show that most stonecutters were not Venetian. They came from further north, from the Ticino canton of modern Switzerland, or from near Lake Como, or had worked in Lombardy and Milan. The route by which the Gothic style was imported into Italy from the north and eventually reached Venice can be traced in these locales. The building obviously subject to the greatest elaboration, and consequently most revealing of these foreign influences, falls outside our study. Suffice it to say that, once the fourteenth-century building had been completed, the Doge's Palace had a far-reaching influence, in its tracery and other details, on the domestic architecture of Gothic Venice.

Once again, it is the waterfront or principal façade that reveals most about domestic architecture and its development in Venice. The photographs of each Gothic façade included in this survey should be studied with attention in order to see the range of inventiveness displayed by the stonecutter in the tracery and carved detail. Though the lacy intricacies of French Flamboyant or English Perpendicular Gothic were never much imitated in conservative Venice, the detail of her Gothic decoration is often extraordinarily fine and Venice still contains the largest number of Gothic secular buildings in the world.

The arch types and tracery of early Venetian Gothic can be illustrated best in the above-mentioned Palazzo Sagredo and, at the latest period, with the intricate tracery of the Palazzo Bernardo (1440s). At the Sagredo house, Ruskin's third arch type appears in the lower *piano nobile* windows. The presence of the fourth type indicates the later date of the lateral addition to the house. The fifth of Ruskin's six arch types is found in the windows of the floor above—the *piano nobile* proper. Fine examples of the sixth type of arch, doubly inflected and surmounted by a carved finial, appear in the façade of the fifteenth-century Palazzo Bernardo. The most elaborate tracery in Venice is that of the Golden House, the Ca' d'Oro. It is a product of the Raverti-Bon workshop of Milanese-Ticinese stonecutters, who adapted and refined forms and patterns from the ducal palace. But the tracery most widely used in Venice was the simpler quatrefoil piercing of an Istrian stone circle placed directly above its supporting column. This too is derived from the tracery of the Doge's Palace.

Like the arch types, the capitals used in Gothic palaces give us an approximate idea of the date of the house. Again, Ruskin's gradation of types from the simple to the elaborate is perhaps the best available. Basically, however, Venetian Gothic capitals can be divided into two types: the earlier has single stylized fronds at each corner, with rosettes decorating the plain flat surfaces between; the second is of a later date and has deeply carved and convoluted leafy foliage wrapped around the capital to give it a full roundness.

Introduction

The balconies of the Gothic house are also of two types. Those inserted flush between the columns consist of balustrades and are called *poggioli*; more rarely they consist of marble panels known as *plutei*. Many of these two types have been removed to allow easy access to projecting balconies added by the owners at a later date, often at the expense of the proportions of the windows and often, too, breaking up the horizontal string courses and mouldings of the façade. The second type, the projecting balcony (probably not introduced before the fifteenth century), was supported on stone brackets elaborately carved with lion's heads, which were meant to be appreciated by those arriving by gondola. The Gothic balcony-rail columnettes have no base and are usually plain shafts without entasis; occasionally miniature leafy capitals join them to the Istrian stone rail. The outer corners of the balcony were frequently decorated with small stone lions *sejant*, occasionally supporting a shield. The traditional upright position of these heraldic animals suggests that they may have been used as posts for securing the outer edge of an awning or sunshade. Few original Gothic balconies survive. A fine example is that on the first *piano nobile* of the Palazzo Barbaro, where the lion's-head brackets are especially well carved. The most elaborately carved of Venetian Gothic balconies are those on the tiny Palazzo Contarini-Fasan. Their design may have derived from details of the Flamboyant Gothic of Milan cathedral and it is significant for the fundamental conservatism of Venetian Gothic taste that these beautiful but elaborate exercises in circular tracery were never repeated.

Another distinctively Gothic feature of the Venetian palace is the use of Istrian stone quoins to frame the façade. These quoins were often carved at their edges with cable moulding or with a simple round moulding with a capital and base to suggest an elongated column. The latter motif became very common, and the single columnar corner moulding was divided in three to correspond with the floors of the house. With cable moulding used horizontally as a string-course, the Gothic façade was thus divided into three oblong compositional sections. The aesthetic achievement of the architect should be understood in terms of these horizontal sections; in fact, this horizontalism is one of the distinguishing features of not only Venetian, but Italian Gothic architecture in general. For example, the top floor of the Foscari palace should be appreciated as a horizontal unit complete in itself in terms of symmetry and decoration, otherwise it appears a top-heavy if not superfluous adjunct to the rest of the façade. It was not until the generation of Sansovino and Sanmicheli that the whole façade began to be considered a compositional unit and even then the horizontal emphasis remained strong.

Although Gothic detail brought about a new style in decoration, many elements from the Veneto-Byzantine palaces remained popular. Round plaques of precious marbles with a small stone sphere projecting on an iron rod from the centre of the plaque were a decorative feature of both the Gothic and earlier periods. These plaques and roundels merit attention because they underline two fundamentally Venetian qualities apparent in more than one of her art forms: chiaroscuro light and colour. The spheres cast shadows and

20. Gothic balcony lion *sejant,* with the Fondaco dei Turchi across the canal

21. The alternating Istrian stone quoins and the richly carved cable-moulding on the façade of Palazzo Contarini-Fasan

break up the flatness of otherwise unrelieved wall space. Depth-giving shadow was also the reason Istrian stone continued to be popular even after finer marbles could be easily obtained. The surface of Istrian stone protected from the weather turns black, thus accentuating the façade's shadows, while the exposed part is washed a bright white. The Venetian love of colour is a well-known cliché of the history of her painting and it is just as true of her architecture. The many frescoed façades have almost entirely vanished, but the coloured marble plaques, now faded by time and dirt, remain as a reminder of this abiding element of the Venetian aesthetic. The many coloured columns of the Basilica appear on a less extravagant scale in the house façades as well, especially in the central group of openings, which lit the *portego* of the *piano nobile*. Obvious examples are found at the Palazzo Foscari and the Palazzo Barbaro, where the central shaft has been identified as marble of the classical Greek period.

The parapet atop the Ca' d'Oro is evidently derived from the Veneto-Byzantine tradition, though its immediate prototype was the roof decoration of the Doge's Palace. Indeed, a great deal of the decoration of that most flamboyant of Venetian Gothic façades is Byzantine in inspiration. The carved borders and friezes of animals and plant life, originally picked out in the gold that gave the house its popular name, are evidence of the continuity of Byzantine aesthetic conventions. Structurally, too, the Ca' d'Oro can be related to the Veneto-Byzantine palace which, in part, it incorporates. Instead of the pointed-arch doorway water-gate common to most Gothic palaces, the Ca' d'Oro has an arcade. The central of its five openings is not only larger than the others, in the Byzantine style, but is surmounted by a round arch, common to the Veneto-Byzantine *curia*. The water entrance of a Gothic palace was generally a simple doorway, either pointed or with a flat lintel stone, and for various reasons it is often difficult to tell if these doors are contemporary with the rest of the building. The water-gate door opened directly into the *andron*, but in Gothic palaces such as the Palazzo Bernardo, which seems to have been designed as a two-family house (or rather, for two branches of the same family), twin water-gates opened into parallel *androni*, which led to two separate courtyards at the back of the house.

The single-family palace courtyard with its external staircase is best illustrated by the Ca' d'Oro, while the double courtyard scheme survives at the Bernardo and Soranzo–Van Axel houses. Of course these courtyards, whether double or single, also had land-side entrances. The land-portal was often not only remarkably large, but also highly decorated, whereas the pointed-arch water-door was very simple and unadorned by comparison. Handsome examples of the land-gates survive in Venice even where the original courtyard or the palace itself has disappeared. Among those still to be found set in high, brick courtyard walls are the land-gates of the Ca' d'Oro, the Foscari, Bernardo, and Soranzo–Van Axel palaces. The Soranzo palace at the Miracoli still has its original Gothic wooden door with a fine knocker. The prominence of the land-gate in the Gothic period (all trace of earlier such gates has disappeared) indicates the patrician owner's sense of position *vis-à-vis* his humbler neighbours. Many people who lived near the palace were his retainers or dependants, and their houses often bore his coat of arms. His arms, carved in stone, were prominently displayed above the land entrance to his house, and high above some *calli* there still exist pointed Gothic arches that served as a kind of boundary marker, decorated with the neighbouring patrician's escutcheon.

The brick wall of the Gothic palace courtyard was often surmounted by a decorative hybrid between the Byzantine and Gothic parapet with a kind of fancy brickwork castellation. Within the courtyard, two features were prominent and traditional: the well-head, or *vera da pozzo*, often carved of Verona marble with foliage motifs borrowed from the Gothic capital, and the external staircase. The structure and function of the external staircase has already been discussed and is only mentioned again to emphasize that it was a distinctly Gothic feature. External staircases undoubtedly existed in the Veneto-Byzantine palaces as well, but hardly any trace of them survives. The Gothic external staircase ended in the *liagò*, or covered porch, which has also been described earlier. The usual place for the *liagò* was therefore at the back of the house. But this particularly Gothic feature might appear elsewhere as well. Twin *liagò* exist on top of two block-like projections from the waterfront façade of the Falier house at San Vidal. These are now glassed in, but in their outline they are very similar to the now vanished *liagò* of the patriarch of Grado's palace near the Rialto, which figures in Carpaccio's great narrative painting for the Scuola Grande di San Giovanni Evangelista.

Beside all that has been described above, the general decoration of the Venetian Gothic palace contains elements that would be recognizably Gothic in any context. There is no need to dwell on the various motifs common to the Gothic stonecutter of Italy: the pointed arches, the foils of tracery, the widely used dentil and rope moulding, the rosettes and other carved stone decorations that punctuated the brick façade of the Gothic house. But one way in which these elements were used was distinctively Venetian. A single window or even the *portego* group of windows was often framed in a rectangle of dentil moulding, and the resulting area of wall space was colourfully filled with variegated marble slabs or a vividly pigmented plaster. These areas break up the flatness of the Venetian Gothic façade and provide another example of the colourism so typical of the arts of the Republic.

Renaissance architecture in Venice is generally considered to have begun with the ceremonial land-gate of the great shipbuilding and armaments complex of the Arsenal. It was built by Antonio Gambello and its date – 1460 – is indicative of the late arrival of the Renaissance in Venice. Donatello had worked in the territories of the Republic a generation earlier and in 1433 Michelozzo had built a library for the monks of San Giorgio Maggiore at the behest of Cosimo de' Medici. But these and other proponents of the Florentine Renaissance had little impact in Venice and produced no immediate followers. It is typical of Venetian conservatism and eclecticism

22. One of the two covered terraces or *liagò* of Palazzo Falier at San Vidal

23. OVERLEAF LEFT The Gothic water-gate and seventeenth-century mezzanine balconies of the Palazzo Zorzi

24. OVERLEAF RIGHT View of the façade of Palazzo Zorzi on the rio di San Lorenzo

Introduction

that the capitals of Gambello's triumphal arch were not imitations of the classical order, as might have been expected, but were original eleventh-century capitals of Byzantine design.

The palaces of the Venetian Renaissance stand markedly apart from the mainstream revival of classical architectural principles and practice. Once again, the peculiar characteristics of the city were a determinant factor. The flat waterfront façade, which made the most of the restricted space available, could not be abandoned in order to demonstrate newly popular concepts of volume, depth, and perspective. Nor could the Venetian architect hope to imitate or reproduce an architectural style based on building in stone. The classical orders of the Roman temple were used in Venetian palaces in much the same way that Gothic tracery or stonework was: as a decorative adjunct to what remained a distinctively local type of building. Renaissance architectural theory had little or no practical application in Venetian domestic architecture and in fact, Venice herself, as opposed to the nearby university city of Padua, was particularly lacking in men who approached the arts along the lines suggested by the humanists. Venetian Renaissance architects were not so much theoreticians like Brunelleschi or Alberti as they were still stonecutters in the Gothic tradition. Of course, their stonecutting and carved decoration incorporated some of the latest innovations and they began to emerge as distinct personalities with particular styles just like any other Renaissance architect, but the high incidence, in even later generations, of sculptors practising architecture in Venice can be partially interpreted as a continuance of the Gothic tradition.

The first recognizably Renaissance architects in Venice were members of the Solaro da Carona family. Like many of the stonecutter-architects who had flourished in Venice in the Gothic period, they came from the Ticino in Switzerland. In the history of Venetian architecture, they are called the Lombardo family and their distinctive style is known as Lombardesque. The confusion with the architecture of Lombardy is partially intentional as they did work in that province and certain characteristics of their style might be described as Lombard in origin. The founder of the dynasty, Pietro (*c.* 1435–1515), arrived in Padua some time in the middle of the century and worked there with the first generation of Donatello's followers. It was there that he absorbed the lessons of the Tuscan Renaissance, though some scholars suppose that he had already visited Florence itself. Around 1467 he came to settle in Venice, where he and his two sons, Tullio (died 1532) and Antonio (died 1516?), established their workshop. They collaborated with Giovanni Buora of Lugano (died 1513) on at least one of their public commissions, the Scuola Grande di San Marco.

Among the Lombardesque palaces in Venice, the Palazzo Dario is attributed to the Lombardi and the Palazzo Contarini-Polignac to Giovanni Buora. The accuracy of these attributions is not important, for it is the Lombardesque style as a whole that is significant in the development of Venetian architecture. Most distinctive was the emphasis on colour and finely

25. An engraving of Palazzo Vendramin-Calergi (Visentini: *Venetian Palaces,* I, British Museum)

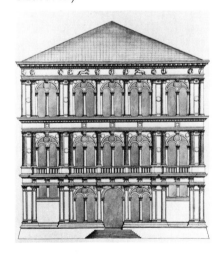

26. Codussian window on the ground floor of the Scuola Grande di San Rocco

carved decoration in low relief. Roundels and plaques of precious marbles became decorative units in themselves and were larger than those found in Gothic façades. At the Palazzo Dario they are framed in an intertwining arabesque complex of smaller plaques and borders. These patterns were obviously inspired by the inlaid marble and tesserae mosaic floors of Venice such as the ones to be seen at the Basilica of San Marco and in the churches of Murano and Torcello. Dividing each floor of the Palazzo Dario is a frieze, which is not treated in a classical manner, but divided into *plutei*-like sections, each decorated with a round marble plaque. Much of the decorative detail of the Lombardesque style can be linked with both the Gothic and Veneto-Byzantine styles. The predominantly Renaissance elements are the round arches and the pilasters carved in bas-relief and capped by capitals of the type popularized in the pseudo-classical architecture of early sixteenth-century painting. Beside the richly carved bas-relief vase and vine motifs of the pilasters and the classically derived mouldings at the Palazzo Contarini-Polignac, there is a fine frieze at the *piano nobile* with the Contarini's heraldic eagles displayed between festoons, as well as a finely carved interpretation of a correctly composed cornice.

In the late fifteenth century, when the Venetian architect might have begun to give more prominence, or at least bring more accuracy, to his employment of classical elements, Mauro Coducci (1440–1504) arrived in Venice. Arguably the city's most distinctive and individual early Renaissance architect, Coducci came from Bergamo, another fount of the Gothic stone-cutter-architect tradition, bringing with him the lately assimilated novelties of the Florentine, Leon Battista Alberti. In Coducci's Corner-Spinelli and Vendramin-Calergi palaces, the distinctive Codussian window (two round-arched lights framed in a larger round arch with a circular or drop-shaped piercing set like tracery in the spandrel) recalls the Tuscan prototype evolved by Alberti for the façade of the Palazzo Rucellai in Florence. But even more Albertian is the rhythmic regularity Coducci imposed on the traditional tripartite Venetian palace façade. The isolation of the central or *portego* windows is partially disguised by the use of attached columns, whose intervals are adjusted or doubled to give the appearance of a regular classical colonnade. The cornices of Coducci's palaces have a classical air and are made to project boldly in Florentine fashion, though the frieze decoration and pilasters are still carved with an unclassical, Lombardesque delicacy. Coducci continued to use the marble plaques as decorative accents; and as a further measure of his truly Venetian eclecticism, the trefoil-plan projecting balconies of the Corner-Spinelli are copied from a late Gothic house in Vicenza, the casa Pigafetta.

This typically Venetian mixture of the new classicism with older elements can be seen, too, on the façade of the Palazzo Contarini delle Figure, attributed to the Milanese, Antonio Abbondi (1505–49), known as Lo Scarpagnino. Built sometime between 1504 and 1546, the aedicular side windows and the antique fluted columns supporting a temple-like pediment above the *portego* windows represent one of the earliest concerted attempts to

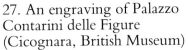

27. An engraving of Palazzo Contarini delle Figure (Cicognara, British Museum)

integrate Roman classical temple forms with the rectangular form and tripartite division of the traditional Venetian palace. But Ruskin was correct in observing the legacy of Gothic stonecutting in the finely carved trophies on the same façade. And once again, the decorative plaques, beribboned in the Lombardesque fashion, and the pilaster divisions of the façade's compartments show the enduring influence of earlier periods and styles. It is significant, too, that an architect of this date, though classicizing in some details, is not interested, as was the Tuscanized Coducci, in disguising the component divisions of the traditional Venetian façade.

Michele Sanmicheli (1484–1559), the great architect of fortification from Verona, also respected the basic Venetian formula in the earliest palace attributed to him in Venice, the Palazzo Gussoni-Grimani. A few conservative classical touches, such as the segmental pediments and the fine proportions of the façade, are all that remains of what must have been a remarkable feature of the Grand Canal. The entire façade was frescoed by Jacopo Tintoretto and his workshop. The abundant wall space of the Gothic or Lombardesque façade was again used at the Palazzo Gussoni-Grimani and provided Tintoretto with a suitable canvas for his personal contribution to the colourism of Venetian architectural tradition.

On the other hand, the palace which Sanmicheli began in 1540 for the Grimani family at San Luca is a massive and resounding statement of Roman High Renaissance classicism. The traditional tripartite disposition is completely disguised in a way reminiscent of Coducci's solution for the Vendramin-Calergi. The lateral windows of the *piano nobile* are separated from the *portego* group by doubled columns. Instead of using the same window-type for the width of the façade, Sanmicheli separates the three immense round-arched openings with rectangular windows, each having a half-size rectangular opening above. The *portego* group is thus actually lit by a modified Serlian group, though the ABABA rhythm of the whole suggests a continuum rather than a three-part composite. The volume, general proportions, and projecting cornice of the Palazzo Grimani suggest further comparison with Coducci's Vendramin-Calergi, but above the *piano nobile* the building was finished by another hand and, on close inspection, only too obviously so. What is remarkably un-Venetian is Sanmicheli's treatment of the water-gate. A triple entrance leads to a barrel-vaulted atrium with flat-ceilinged side aisles like Sangallo's entrance to the Palazzo Farnese in Rome. It is an impressive and imaginative use of the space dictated by the traditional *andron* and though the conservative Venetians did not copy it immediately, Baldassare Longhena used a modified version of the idea much later in two of his grandest palaces. Sanmicheli's balanced use of finely conceived classical elements, emphasizing every possible contrast in depth and volume on a flat façade, resulted in one of the architecturally most interesting palaces of Venice. For all that and perhaps because of its bold, foreign air, the conservative Venetians adopted hardly any of its most distinctive features.

One feature, however, was taken from Sanmicheli's design for the Grimani

28. The courtyard end of Palazzo Barbaro's *portego* and a handsome *Kachelofen*

29. An engraving of the façade of Palazzo Grimani (Cicognara, British Museum)

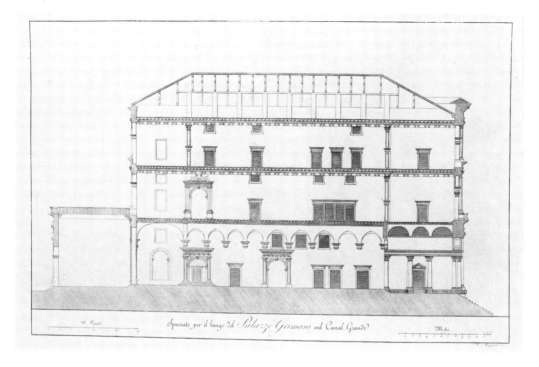

30. An engraving of Palazzo Grimani

house and was widely used in the sixteenth and seventeenth centuries in quite a different context. This was the *portego* BAB group of windows: the Serlian group with square windows placed above the lateral rectangular openings. Sanmicheli's *Serliana* was first adapted by Giangiacomo Grigi (died 1572), who had completed the upper floors of the Grimani house. The façade of his Palazzo Papadopoli is a curtain wall of Istrian stone with none of the volumes, mass, or chiaroscuro effects of Sanmicheli's façade. Yet the central element is unmistakably Sanmicheli's *Serliana* interpreted in plain pilasters instead of full fluted Corinthian columns. Grigi's flat, conservative façade with its central Serlian motif and lateral pedimented windows proved extremely popular with the Venetians. The sixteenth-century Palazzo Mocenigo and Longhena's Palazzo Giustinian are almost exact copies of it, while Vittoria's Palazzo Balbi and a host of others can be related to it.

Sanmicheli's near-contemporary, Jacopo Tatti of Florence, called Sansovino (1486–1570), was even more influential in shaping Venetian Renaissance taste in building. In his capacity as *protomagister* of San Marco, or architect to the Republic, Sansovino was at his most inventive and elaborate. His astonishing versatility can be seen in the fortress-like strength of the State Mint, the delicacy and colourism of the pretty *loggetta* at the base of the *campanile*, and the sculpturism of the Marciana Library, which Palladio described as the richest building built since classical times. In the two palaces considered here, the native conservatism of Sansovino's private patrons is evident. He never attempted a palace as fundamentally un-Venetian as Sanmicheli's house for the Grimani at San Luca.

The first of Sansovino's two palaces was built for the Dolfin family near the Rialto and is now known as the Palazzo Manin; it is a restrained classical exercise. The open arcade of Tuscan semi-columns has often been regarded as a striking innovation in Venetian architecture; in reality, it is merely an elegant treatment of the traditional Venetian *sottoportego*. The rest of the façade rather reverses the trend begun by Coducci and carried further by Sanmicheli: Sansovino emphasizes the wall space rather than practically eliminating it altogether. In Coducci's Vendramin palace and Sanmicheli's Palazzo Grimani the subtle and elaborate treatment of the window units and the adjustment of the columnar intervals reduced the wall space to virtual insignificance. Sansovino's austere façade for the Dolfin house stands in contrast to the spirit of those two houses and to much of what he himself built later. The huge, solemn villa which Sansovino built for the Garzoni family at Pontecasale near Padua seems closest to the Dolfin façade in both austerity and proportions. There was, of course, considerable cross-fertilization between the architects of Sansovino's own and the preceding generations, and the frieze at the Palazzo Dolfin with its widely spaced lion's heads clearly recalls the rhythms of the Lombardesque frieze at the Vendramin-Calergi.

At the Palazzo Corner della Ca' Grande, the influence of Sanmicheli seems more prominent, though the order of influence is difficult to determine since both houses were being built at about the same time. Sansovino designed a triple water-gate entrance for the Corner, though he was not so un-Venetian as to construct a barrel-vaulted atrium behind it. He also used rustication for the ground-floor Istrian stone facing, a hall-mark of Sanmicheli's building in Verona and Coducci's Corner-Spinelli palace in Venice, but also possibly a result of Sansovino's Tuscan background and Roman training. The prominence given to this wall space accords with his earlier treatment at the Palazzo Dolfin, but the upper floors return to the ideas of Coducci and the Grimani house. Doubled attached columns, adjusted to disguise the tripartite intervals of the *piano nobile*, create the appearance of a continuous, regular

31. An engraving of Palazzo Corner della Ca'Grande

arcade. The entablature above is no longer treated as a plain frieze on which to display decorative or heraldic motifs, but is pierced with oval openings to light the attic floor – a motif taken from the architect's own treatment of the Libreria attic.

With the Palazzo Corner, Sansovino established a virtual canon for a later generation of architects and especially for that most Venetian architect of the Baroque period, Baldassare Longhena. The triple water-entrance arches; the rusticated ground-floor walls; balconies fitted to the windows above a cornice which clearly marks the horizontal divisions of the façade; the use of double columns and adjusted intervals to achieve an apparently regular distribution of the windows on the principal floors; spandrels filled with sculpture; prominently carved head or mask keystones for the window arches, and an attic pierced with oval openings: all these are characteristic of Sansovino's contribution to Venetian palace architecture. Yet despite the wide range of his contribution, the plan and layout as well as the basic volumes of the Venetian palace still remained fundamentally unaltered. Sansovino's most significant modification of the basic Venetian palace type was the introduction of a courtyard incorporated in the fabric, first at the Palazzo Dolfin and then at the Palazzo Corner. Given the unusually large building site provided him by the Corner, Sansovino's courtyard is an impressive part of the palace, though more Roman in feeling than Venetian. This courtyard was not fully assimilated into the vocabulary of Venetian palace building until the lavish Baroque period, when the palace swallowed the whole building site, and gardens virtually disappeared or were treated as of little importance.

Whereas Sansovino, Sanmicheli and, earlier, Coducci had attempted to introduce in the façade a Renaissance classical vocabulary of decoration, and of varying and contrasting surfaces and volumes which would give the impression of regularity, depth, and variety, there was also a contrasting tendency in Venetian architecture, best represented by the influence of Grigi's Palazzo Papadopoli, where the façade was treated as a flat surface, with its traditional tripartite divisions clearly marked and decorated with sculpturesque rather than architectonic accents. Alessandro Vittoria (1524–1608), adapting Grigi's flat façade, introduced at the Palazzo Balbi highly mannerist motifs of decoration, such as the broken pediments above the lateral windows, the prominent heraldic cartouches of the *piano nobile*, and free-standing paired Ionic columns for the *portego* windows, reminiscent of Giulio Romano's mannerist arcade for the Palazzo del Tè at Mantua. Vittoria had worked for the Barbaro brothers at Maser along with Palladio, and his architecture represents a similar amalgam of classicism breaking off into a mannerist expression. Palladio made several designs for Venetian palaces and it is interesting that, un-Venetian as they were, they followed the style of Grigi in the flatness and clear divisions of their façades. None of these projects of Palladio was ever executed, but it is remarkable that they are so different in feeling from the palaces he built in Vicenza, and that they did not follow the work of Sanmicheli, who had had such an influence on his other palace

32. An engraving of the façade of Palazzo Contarini degli Scrigni (Cicognara, British Museum)

designs. There can be little doubt that Palladio, like most architects who worked in Venice, took account of her conservatism in building taste. His disciple, Vicenzo Scamozzi (1552–1616), was given several important commissions in Venice, including that of completing Sansovino's Library on the Piazzetta, but he built only one palace in the city, the Palazzo Contarini degli Scrigni. Though not particularly pleasing, it does illustrate the treatment of the Venetian façade as a curtain wall space as opposed to a frame space for arcading and subtle window and column combinations intended to give the illusion of depth and volume. Scamozzi was a theorist of classical purism. He seems to have taken his passion for classical regularity to an extreme when he opened only one window where the *portego* group should be, but the function of this building should be understood before Scamozzi's treatment is dismissed as a mere solecism. The 'Scrigni' palace is an extension of the Gothic Contarini-Corfu house, and its width provides reception rooms for the earlier house. Hence, in plan, it does not follow the traditional layout. Just as several generations were to pass before Sansovino's ideas at the Corner were fully adopted and transformed by Baroque architects, Scamozzi's classical restraint did not come into its own until the neoclassical phase of eighteenth-century building.

The Venetian Baroque style is as individualistically Venetian as were the styles of the Gothic and Renaissance periods. The Doge's Palace of the Gothic period, Sansovino's Renaissance Libreria and Longhena's extraordinary and unique church, Santa Maria della Salute, well illustrate the peculiarly Venetian results achieved by architects representative of those periods and fashions. Like most other manifestations of the Baroque, Venetian Baroque was heavily charged with decoration, but on palace façades this no longer meant a painterly application of touches of colour, or the use of fine bas-relief, or a smattering of barely assimilated classical elements. The lessons of Sansovino and the Palazzo Grimani had been well absorbed and mass, volume, depth, and movement determined the nature of the most impressive Venetian Baroque decoration. All this meant an extensive use of stone, and deeply carved Istrian stone rustication is as characteristic of the Venetian Baroque palace as anything else. In the interiors, the more conservative taste of earlier periods was now disregarded and exuberantly theatrical stucco-work became popular; furniture by master *ébénistes* such as Brustolon and Corradini were as much works of sculpture as they were chairs or consoles; elaborate Murano chandeliers decorated the long, open space of the *portego*. None the less, certain elements of a Venetian conservatism do persist.

In one of his early palaces, the Palazzo Giustiniani-Lolin, the Venetian Baroque master architect, Baldassare Longhena (1598–1692), remained faithful to the conservative school of Grigi, whereas at the Palazzo Belloni-Battagia he applies the lessons of Vittoria's mannerist work at the Palazzo Balbi and begins the transformation to his own distinctive Baroque idiom. This came to full flower in the work he began and the plans he left for the Rezzonico and Pesaro palaces. Both these houses were completed by other architects in the eighteenth century, and in the upper floors, especially of the Rezzonico, an incipient restraint can be felt. But for the rest, Longhena's idiom was one of rich, deep carving. Architectural elements borrowed from Sansovino and Sanmicheli were made more sculpturesque and gave his buildings a tremendous feeling of movement, chiaroscuro, and volume. Sansovino's canon of a rusticated ground floor, a triple-arched water-entrance leading to a courtyard, and a regular progression of *piano nobile* windows with doubled columns disguising the tripartite façade divisions, is seen at its most elaborate at the Palazzo Pesaro. Heavily carved balustrades, grotesque masks, and an extensive use of rusticated columns are distinctive features of Longhena's style. The Ca' Rezzonico could be considered a slightly more restrained anticipation of the themes of the Palazzo Pesaro, but both must have seemed ostentatious; and though both palaces may be seen as the culmination of Venice's most important and original architectural traditions, no other palaces were built in Venice with such lavish use of stone decoration. *Pietra d'Istria* was still used to cover the façades of other seventeenth- and eighteenth-century palaces, but in slabs rather than in the heavy blocks required for Longhena's rustication and sculptural decoration. It is significant that one of the few palaces planned in the Longhena mode after that architect's death, the Palazzo Venier dei Leoni, was never completed for lack of funds. The eighteenth-century Labia palace has only one of its two façades completed with a richness of detail and stonework that might approach the extravagance of the Longhena school; the other façade is markedly plainer.

Most of Venice's seventeenth- and eighteenth-century palaces were built on much less extravagant lines than the importance of Longhena's achievement might suggest. This phenomenon need not be solely ascribed to the declining financial fortunes of the Republic, for ancient families recently re-enriched, such as the Pisani at Santo Stefano, still chose to erect immense buildings as their *casa domenicale*. Just the same, the Palazzo Pisani remains somewhat exceptional. It was the result of the collaboration of a series of architects of the seventeenth and early eighteenth centuries and grew to such dimensions that the Senate actually forbade its completion – a last noteworthy instance of the Republic's abiding suspicion of a single family's pre-eminence or excessive ostentation. The Pisani's ostentation is not immediately apparent in the campo façade, which is indeed large, but of a fairly restrained design and covered with flat slabs of Istrian stone. It is the double courtyard that indicates the scale of their ambition, just as their vast villa on the Brenta reflected the immensity of their banking fortune. Not only is the courtyard at Santo Stefano richly paved, finished, and decorated in classical style, but it is divided in two by a four-storey architectural screen which provides a passageway between two wings of the house. Such a screen seems no more than theatrical in a palace like the Palazzo Borghese in Rome, where immense courtyards had long existed and where the wings of a palace could meander for acres; but in Venice, where building space was at a premium, an elaborate building used only as a passageway was the height of extravagance.

33. Furniture by A. Brustolon (late seventeenth-century) against the Crosato frescoes in the ballroom at Palazzo Rezzonico

More typical of post-Longhena palaces in Venice were the late seventeenth-century buildings of Antonio Gaspari (1670–1730) and his circle, represented here by the long, plain rio façade of the Palazzo Zenobio and the tall Albrizzi house, where the flat surfaces are covered not with stone, but with a less costly *intonaco*. At this period, it was the interior on which expense was lavished, as can be seen in the impressive ballroom added by Gaspari to the Palazzo Barbaro. This type of addition to a Gothic palace recalls Scamozzi's work for the Contarini and coincidentally, it was at this period that Scamozzi's two-dimensional, neoclassical treatment of the Venetian façade, formulated over a century earlier, began to come into its own.

Two noteworthy examples of the mature neoclassical taste are the Palazzo Valmarana-Mangilli, whose new façade was designed by Antonio Visentini (1688–1782), and the Palazzo Grassi. The architect of the latter was Giorgio Massari (1686–1776), a Venetian, who had completed the upper floors of Ca' Rezzonico. Despite his fidelity to Longhena's designs, Massari's restraint shows in the attic floor and frieze of the Rezzonico, where the decoration has been virtually flattened into the frieze. The entire façade of the Grassi house is also handled in a two-dimensional manner. The orders, correctly Doric, Ionic, and Corinthian, are expressed in plain pilasters rather than columns. The rhythm of the *piano nobile* windows recalls the work of the young Sansovino at the Palazzo Dolfin-Manin, where wall space gave emphasis to the traditional tripartite Venetian façade.

Palazzo Grassi is a remarkable building in many ways. Not only is it one of the earliest expressions of neoclassical restraint in Venice, but it also stands witness to the virtuosity of an architect who could complete the great Longhena's work with fidelity to detail and spirit and yet build in his own distinctive idiom. More incidentally, the Palazzo Grassi illustrates how even the most consciously theoretical Venetian architects built with the exigencies of particular sites in mind. The Palazzo Grassi has a campo façade that is visible, owing to the shape of the site, from the Grand Canal, and Massari therefore adjusted all the projecting details on this side façade so that they would appear regular from the canal. The balconies and their supporting brackets all bend toward the water.

The water-gate atrium and courtyard of the Palazzo Grassi give a grand and open appearance to the ground floor and indicate that the practical or even earlier commercial function of the traditional *andron* had all but disappeared by the eighteenth century. At the back of the courtyard, a monumental staircase on an open plan, with a single flight rising to a long landing and then returning to the *piano nobile* in two flights, further emphasizes the palatial stateliness required by the *arriviste* or newly rich patrician. The Rezzonico had a *Treppenhaus* and ballroom added to their house; the enlarged Palazzo Pisani incorporated several ballrooms; the Zenobio's *portego* was T-shaped to contain a proper ballroom with musicians' balconies and they had an elaborate Baroque pavilion built at the foot of their parterred gardens. Yet in all these houses, despite their un-Venetian accretions and additions, the basic elements

Introduction

of the traditional palace type can still be discerned. Many other palaces, of lesser interest to any save the specialist, were still being built well into the eighteenth century according to the traditional plan. In fact, most of the houses here representing palace building in the last two centuries of the Republic's millennial history are not typical of the majority of Venetian palaces. They are rather the exceptions, and as such are, of course, exceptionally interesting, especially since they are products of such fertile and original geniuses as Scamozzi, Longhena, Visentini, and Massari.

The end of the Republic in 1797 also marked the end of the tradition of Venetian palace building. The patriciate as an institution conferring both privilege and responsibility was destroyed. Its financial foundations had long since begun to erode, first with the circumnavigation of Africa and the subsequent by-passing of the Mediterranean due to the development of northern and transatlantic trade routes; then with the growing hegemony of Turkish naval power in the eastern Mediterranean and the eventual loss of the profitable colonial empire to the infidel. But as is always true in history, the picture cannot be painted in black and white. Some Venetian trade and banking still flourished, and the state revenues towards the end of the eighteenth century have been calculated, even in the inflated currency of the day, to have been healthy. But Napoleon put an end to whatever financial hopes the patriciate may have had, and was true to his promise to be an 'Attila for the Venetian State'. During the brief Regno Italico (1805–15), his agents razed to the ground at least eighty Venetian churches and some forty palaces. This barbarism is generally overlooked and the visitor is fed instead on the anti-Austrian propaganda of the Risorgimento.

The Austrians were disliked in Venice, it is true, as it is only natural for the natives of an occupied country to dislike any occupying force. But for the first twenty years of Austrian rule, Venice was governed with liberalism and justice; better and more equably governed than England in the same period according to the historian G. M. Trevelyan. The Venetians were irritated by the Austrian bureaucracy and the restrictions imposed on them, but the real problem was, and to a great extent still is, that the city had become impoverished by a concatenation of historical and economic factors, and was unable to recover even a shadow of her former glory. In a way, all this was providential. Venice preserved her unique aristocratic beauty through a century that disfigured so many other towns with the marks of bourgeois prosperity and machine-produced vulgarity. Her palaces remained intact, though crumbling, and enough of her remaining patricians married into wealthy Austrian families to ensure the preservation of some of the riches of bygone days. Friezes and ceilings were not always sold off with the movable treasures, and collections of eighteenth-century furniture may still be found *in situ*. What was sold by most of the families was sold for survival. Hardly any of the palaces were redecorated in nineteenth-century taste, as no one could afford it. The virtually unique example illustrated here is the seventeenth-century palace of the Emo family, built for the Barozzi at San Moisè, which became the home of the Treves, bankers to the Austrian empire. A splendid example of enlightened early nineteenth-century artistic patronage, the Palazzo Treves is filled with paintings and furniture by the best artists of the period. Two giant statues of Ajax and Hector commissioned from Canova were installed in a room redecorated in neoclassical style by G. B. Meduna (1800–80). Metternich and the Emperor Francis II came to admire their banker's collections. Apart from this hall, the Treves made few significant alterations to the original palace and it remains a monument to the Venice of the Austrian period.

With so many palaces surviving, it might be assumed that there are still innumerable examples of unspoiled interiors. Unfortunately, this is not the case. The earliest interiors have disappeared in the lavish redecoration fashionable in the eighteenth century. There is no lack of interiors of this period, but frequently inferior materials or second-rate artists were employed to achieve as grand an effect as possible in a short time. Besides, many eighteenth-century interiors have been spoiled by being used as offices, schools, and institutions. Neon lighting, metal filing cabinets, and desks have replaced the Murano chandeliers and lacquered furniture of the patrician, and flimsy partitions have ruined the interior proportions. Almost half the palaces in this survey have succumbed to this sort of transformation.

In the nineteenth century, radical redecoration was not common, but the vast rooms of a *piano nobile* were often divided with cumbersome walls, creating cosy rooms but destroying the traditional dimensions. More recently, palaces have been divided into apartments. The palaces that have kept their original structure are, in fact, well suited to this kind of division. Grand, yet self-sufficient flats can be made of the *piano nobile*, and more modest apartments in the spacious attics or the smaller mezzanines. However, hardly any palace survives with only its basic structure. Warrens of rooms have been added at various times, displacing the garden at the back of the house. Many palace gardens have completely disappeared in this way and the few that do survive are usually victims of the neglect of the multiple owners of the divided building.

A Venetian palace of two *piano nobili* might be well divided into five or six apartments, but more often there are twice this number and they tend, like the minor housing of the city, to be of a labyrinthine complexity. Some rooms are in the original palace, with others leading off into the building's later additions and accretions. The difference between this kind of division and the palace that is intelligently divided, preserving something of the original atmosphere, is obviously difficult to illustrate and almost impossible to define since the solutions employed vary from house to house. The illustrations of interiors here are meant to suggest the atmosphere of a patrician house. The variety of details may seem occasionally contradictory, but with the constancy of Venetian conventions and traditions in mind, a composite of the archetypal Venetian interior should be possible to envisage.

Before concluding this rapid survey, it might be of interest to glance at one

Introduction

of the apparent anomalies of Venetian architectural history: there is no palace in Venice built to the designs of Andrea Palladio. This architect, whose plans and fragments of palaces still existing in Vicenza continue to fascinate architectural historians and students, did draw up plans for at least one house in Venice. But bearing in mind the remarks made on preceding pages about the basically conservative and eclectic nature of Venetian building practice, it is easy to guess why Palladio never found a patron for his plans. First, the elevation of the façade shows that he envisaged an extremely tall building, even by the standards of Sansovino's Palazzo Corner della Ca' Grande. The façade is of a severe classicism with no provision for the richer decorative motifs in fashion in the mid-sixteenth century nor any apparent consideration for the traditional tripartite façade and plan. Moreover, Bertotti-Scamozzi's sectional interpretation indicates that Palladio made no provision for mezzanine offices such as were still traditionally an integral part of a *cinquecento* palace. Neither does there appear to have been a proper *portego* – and though the Venetians of the sixteenth century, and even more their successors, accepted the transformation of the *andron* into an atrium leading to an elaborate courtyard, it is less likely that Palladio's transformation of the traditional *piano nobile* plan would have appealed to them. Surely the central portion would have been very dark, especially since the windows at the rear would have been permanently shaded by a loggia. The most original feature of the plan, the staircase, might or might not have appealed to a Venetian, but it may seem significant that no such staircase was built in a Venetian palace until the nineteenth century. Looking at a plan like Palladio's helps one understand the extent to which local traditions and tastes were important in determining the type of palace built at all periods in the Republic's history. Of course, the importance of these elements can be exaggerated, but their continuity in the vocabulary of Venetian architectural history helps to define what is distinctively Venetian, and therefore unique, about the palaces of Venice.

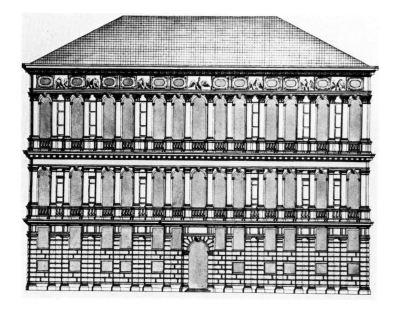

34. An engraving of the façade of Palazzo Labia (Visentini: *Venetian Palaces,* I, British Museum)

BYZANTINE PALACES

Fondaco dei Turchi

The name 'Fondaco (or Fontego in Venetian dialect) dei Turchi', meaning the emporium of the Turkish merchants, applies only to a brief, though colourful period of this building's long life. As a *fondaco*, it would have no place in this study, just as the Fondaco of the Germans at the Rialto is not included, but the original Veneto-Byzantine structure, coldly imitated in the harsh and mechanical nineteenth-century reconstruction, began life some time in the early thirteenth century as a palace. Various sources date it to 1225 and some name a certain Jacopo Palmieri as the man for whom it was built, but it is with his descendants of the Pesaro family that the palace is usually associated. In the earliest records it is described as a *palazzo con curia*, the latter term describing the distinctive Byzantine arcade and loggia which is visible, with its flanking towers or *torreselle*, in Jacopo de' Barbari's view of the city in 1500. But long before 1500, the palace was to change hands many times.

In the late fourteenth century, it was acquired from the Pesaro for 10,000 ducats by the Venetian Republic – both the buyer and the price being sufficient indication of the building's prominence in the city. In 1381, Venice made a gift of the palace to Nicholas V d'Este, marquis of Ferrara. It was in the Palazzo dei Duchi di Ferrara, as the Fondaco was then known, that the Republic decided to house and entertain one of its most illustrious visitors, the Emperor of Byzantium, John VIII Paleologus, who arrived by sea with the patriarch of Constantinople early in February 1438. The emperor's flotilla, in convoy with a single Venetian ship, took over two months to reach Venice, eluding Turkish marauders by passing from the safety of one Venetian port in the eastern Mediterranean to another. The emperor was accompanied by over 650 Orthodox clerics, whose fervent desire for unity with the Church of Rome had inspired this remarkable pilgrimage to the Council of Ferrara, later to be transferred and perhaps better known as the Council of Florence. The riches and hospitality of the Venetian state and the honours paid to the emperor by Doge Francesco Foscari were commented upon by Greeks and Italians alike, and when the customary tributes and protocols had been completed, the emperor departed under Venetian protection, making his way to Ferrara by water.

When the Republic's ambitions on the mainland embroiled her in wars with Ferrara the house was confiscated in 1482. It was again taken from the d'Este during Venice's struggles with the League of Cambrai, and on the Republic's submission to Julius II in 1509, it was awarded to that pope as the residence of his legates. Later in the sixteenth century, it was back in the hands

35. The Fondaco dei Turchi, or emporium of the Turkish merchants, originally a palace of the Pesaro family

61

Fondaco dei Turchi

of the dukes of Ferrara, and in 1549 it was the setting for the baptism of Francesco Maria d'Este, a gathering that reflected not the Republic's politics, but her artistic patrimony. Among the Venetian nobles present was that triumvirate of Venetian artistic taste: Aretino, Titian, and Jacopo Sansovino. During the d'Este tenancy, the house became associated with the names of other of their relations and protégés: Lucrezia Borgia, Torquato Tasso, and Ariosto, all of whom probably knew the palace, even if their sojourns there are not well documented.

In the second half of the sixteenth century, Turkish merchants began to congregate in Venice, and in 1574 it was proposed to the Senate that they should be segregated and housed in a single building. In 1621, the Fondaco was hired for this purpose from the Doge Antonio Priuli, who had bought it for his family some years earlier. To house the Turks, the doors and windows of the palace were blocked to conform with Muslim custom, a mosque and baths were installed, and a restriction was placed on the entry of women. The community was supervised by the *Savii alla Mercanzia*, a committee of the Senate concerned with trade and navigation. In 1627, the Senate ordered the

36. Palazzo Belloni-Battagia (left), the Venetian granary (centre) and the Fondaco dei Turchi (right)

37. Fondaco dei Turchi before restoration (photo Courtauld Institute, London)

destruction of the ancient towers, the *torreselle*, and enacted a series of laws prohibiting the introduction of firearms or gunpowder into the building.

During the early years of its existence as a Turkish emporium, the ownership of the palace reverted to the ancient Pesaro family when, in 1648, the heiress Marietta Priuli married the procurator Leonardo, the builder of the Palazzo Pesaro at San Stae. None the less, it remained a home for the Turks in Venice, undisturbed by either the fortunes of its owners or even, ironically enough, by the fortunes of the Most Serene Republic herself. The Turkish merchants housed in the Fondaco not only survived the collapse of the Republic, they also outstayed Napoleon and were still in residence under the Austrians until 1838, when the last, a certain Saddo-Drisdi, was forced to leave by the Manin family, who had inherited the palace from the Pesaro.

The neglect and decay of this once proud relic of the Republic's political and artistic inheritance from Byzantium raised an outcry from Ruskin when he was in Venice writing his famous study of her early architecture. In 1859, a radical restoration programme was undertaken, financed by 40,000 lire from the municipal authorities and 80,000 florins from the Austrian government. The works were directed by the engineer Frederico Berchet and took ten years to complete. In its details, it is a painfully heavy-handed interpretation of the Veneto-Byzantine original, but on account of its unique role in the city's history it has been included here as an introduction to Venice's domestic architecture.

Palazzo Loredan

The Palazzo Loredan on the riva del Ferro near the Rialto presents a good example of the confusions of Venetian nomenclature. For the better part of the Republic's existence this great palace, the two lower floors of which are ascribed to the Veneto-Byzantine style of the thirteenth century, was known not as the Palazzo Loredan, but as the Palazzo Corner-Piscopia, and its riva, or bank of the canal, was called 'della Moneta'; the riva del Ferro (iron) being then on the opposite shore. Iron, which arrived by river from Germany, was one of Venice's principal exports to the Levant; she traded it for the fabled silks and spices of the Orient.

The site and perhaps the construction of the Palazzo Loredan has been associated with the Boccasi family, originally from Parma, and later with the ancient Venetian Zane or Ziani family, whose doge, Sebastiano, presided over the legendary encounter of the emperor Frederick Barbarossa with the Pope in 1177. By the fourteenth century the palace was inhabited by the Corner family, merchants who claimed an illustrious descent from the Cornelii of imperial Rome and who had enriched themselves after the Fourth Crusade with their holdings in the eastern Mediterranean, especially Cyprus. In 1365 Frederico Corner, known for his wealth as 'il grande', was host here to Peter Lusignan, King of Cyprus, who showed his gratitude for a gift of some 70,000 gold ducats by knighting him. From then on the Corner family proudly displayed the Lusignan arms on the façade of their palace, flanking their own shield with the carved, painted, and gilded attributes of their knighthood: helmet, sword, and motto. Also represented in the frieze are small statues symbolizing Venice and Justice seated on lions under Gothic canopies. At the corners of this frieze stand small carved figures of David and Goliath, representing the triumph of virtue over vice. Whichever of the Corner's virtues triumphed, and it may have been simply the virtue of being rich, the King of Cyprus also invested them with the fief of Piscopia, a castle with extensive lands on the island. Though the government forbade the use of titles in the *Dominante*, this branch of the Corner family adopted their Cypriot distinction as part of their family name.

Vast riches continued to be the distinguishing feature of most branches of the Corner family, and lengthy, if rather repetitious and boring descriptions exist of the dowries and wedding-feasts of their daughters. But the Corner were also noteworthy for their military and administrative prowess. Two Corner called Frederico fought in the Genoese wars and were present with Andrea Contarini at the recapture of Chioggia in 1381. Three members of this

38. Palazzo Loredan at the Rialto – thirteenth-century Veneto-Byzantine architecture

branch were galley captains, one of the highest ranks of the Venetian navy, at the battle of Lepanto in 1571. In the seventeenth century, Giovanni Battista Corner Piscopia was captain at Bergamo, *provveditore* at Peschiera, and in 1649 was made one of the nine procurators of the Republic. Like his ancestor, Frederico il grande, who gave great sums to aid the Republic during the Genoese wars, Giovanni Battista contributed more than 20,000 ducats to the effort against the Turks at Candia in Crete. He also used his fortune to redecorate and embellish his palace at the Rialto, remodelling the courtyard and constructing a magnificent staircase hall. But his most noteworthy contribution to the Republic was to father a remarkable daughter, Elena Corner Piscopia, an accomplished poetess and musician, who received the laurels and ring of a baccalaureate in Aristotelian philosophy at Padua in 1678. Her *viva* had to be conducted in the cathedral, such were the numbers of the curious, and on her return to Venice the Senate met in special session to hear one of her orations. By Elena's day the Palazzo Corner Piscopia was famous for its library as well as for a splendid collection of armour.

In 1703, the palace passed into the Loredan family on the marriage of Lucrezia, last of the Corner Piscopia, to Giovanni Battista Loredan. After one hundred years of Loredan ownership, the palace suffered the degrading fate common to many of the larger houses of Venice. It was for a time a printing plant, a locanda, a stage coach agency, headquarters of the water-bus company, and later of the railways. It returned to private ownership briefly in the nineteenth century, when Contessa Peccona from Verona spent vast sums on redecorating it to a Victorian standard of magnificence, and then passed out of her hands to become an hotel. In 1867 it was bought by the present owners, the municipality of Venice, who restored it again in 1881. These successive nineteenth-century restorations and the present use of the building to house a warren of municipal offices leave hardly a hint of its former glories, to say nothing of its Veneto-Byzantine plan. But the façade with its Byzantine *curia* and its doubled columns to mark the original division between the arcades and the *torreselle* signalled the appearance of a motif that was to influence Venetian architects of almost every generation.

39. Palazzo Loredan and
Palazzo Farsetti

Palazzo Donà della Madonnetta

The handsome *curia* of the *piano nobile* of the small Palazzo Donà della Madonnetta at Sant'Aponal is of sufficient architectural interest in itself to merit inclusion here. However little is otherwise known about the house, this feature alone and the fine proportions of its façade give it an air of authentic antiquity. There is no doubt that it is very old and that it was an integral part of the cluster of merchants' dwellings and places of business, covered by the term *casa fondaco*, that grew up around their principal market and business exchange at the Rialto. The arches of the Donà arcade are definitely of the Veneto-Byzantine type though they are less stilted than the prototypes to be found on earlier buildings such as the eleventh- and twelfth-century churches at Torcello. The Donà house has been dated from the early thirteenth century. In other Veneto-Byzantine houses, the facing of the arches is framed with a double line of dentil moulding, but here there is only one such moulding, which meets above the capital. The rhythms of the arcade are further decorated with tiny paterae set in the spandrels between the arches. Whether the *curia* was originally flanked by the traditional *torreselle* is open to question, but the presence of square piers instead of columns at the extremes of the present arcade suggests some sort of structural division of the façade. Remodelling carried out since the fifteenth century, when the upper loggia was added and the Donatellesque Madonna was set in the façade, makes it difficult to establish or reconstruct the house's original appearance. A branch of the ancient Donato or Donà family lived here, and added to their name a reference to a small shrine of the Madonna which stood in a nearby street. It may have been in this house that Marco Donato lived in the early fourteenth century. It was he who betrayed the conspiracy against the government led by the Querini and Tiepolo families in 1310. Under the banner of Bajamonte Tiepolo a number of disaffected Venetians rose up against the doge Pietro Gradenigo who had, by his disastrous mainland policies, brought Venice under a papal ban of excommunication. The real issues behind the Tiepolo plot were complex and obscure, but the episode quickly assumed a prominent place in the mythology of the Venetian State and also resulted in the formation of a powerful committee of public safety, famous in history as the Council of Ten, designed to uncover and punish cases of treason. For his part in foiling the conspiracy of 1310, Marco Donato and his male issue were admitted to the ranks of the patriciate which had been otherwise closed to the Venetians only a few years before in 1297. Recently Palazzo Donà della Madonnetta has been sensitively restored.

Palazzo da Mosto

40. Byzantine sculpture (John Ruskin: *The Stones of Venice* 1851–53)

The façade of the Veneto-Byzantine palace of the da Mosto family across from the Rialto markets on the Grand Canal is one of the most richly decorated examples of its kind in the city. The profusion of paterae and a delicately carved frieze above the *curia* point to the inextricable links that existed between the secular and ecclesiastical stonecutters, the architects, and the patrons of the day. Paterae are decorative stone plaques carved with symmetrical animal and plant life motifs; they generally had a religious significance, as for example the popular two peacocks drinking from a fountain. According to ancient bestiaries, peacocks were birds of incorruptible flesh and their drinking symbolized eternal life through baptism. Other animals with more recondite significance abound, often framed, as in the frieze of the Palazzo da Mosto, with a carved motif of vines, symbolizing the 'true vine' of St John's Gospel. Paterae were set in walls of churches, perhaps as ex-votos. The hieratic figures of saints, the Redeemer, or even the emperor carved on these plaques suggest a votive intention, and paterae

41. Palazzo da Mosto (centre); the lower two floors are Veneto-Byzantine

69

appeared on secular as well as on ecclesiastical buildings of the Byzantine empire. In Venice they were either carved locally, or in some cases, such as on the Basilica of San Marco, were copies of pieces brought from the east and considered precious enough to be duplicated. It would hardly be accurate to consider them all the booty of conquest and pillaging such as that to which the Venetians and their allies subjected Constantinople in 1204; many may have been purchased or commissioned locally. In any case, they were used prominently in the decoration of Veneto-Byzantine palace façades.

The Palazzo da Mosto is not only a fine example of Veneto-Byzantine architecture, it was also the birthplace of one of the Republic's most famous explorers, Alvise da Mosto (1432–88). As a young man, he was well trained in the twin vocations of the Venetian patrician, commerce and navigation. In 1454, he set off on a trading voyage in the Atlantic, but bad weather interrupted his plans and he was forced into harbour at Cape Saint Vincent. It was there that he met and was fascinated by the projects and personality of the Portuguese prince, Henry the Navigator. He entered the Infante's service and set sail along the coast of Africa. Da Mosto is often credited with the discovery of the Cape Verde islands during this expedition. His Portuguese ships returned home, but he settled in Lagos and, true to his training, he remained for seven years engaged in commerce. By the early 1470s he had returned to Venice and in 1473 participated in the defence of Cattaro, which was being attacked by Turkish forces. In 1481 he commanded a convoy of merchant galleys on their yearly voyage to Alexandria in Egypt. His career well illustrates the patrician's involvement in all types of maritime activity and serves to remind the historian of the degree to which commerce, exploration, and naval strategy were not only in the hands of the same men, but depended on the versatility and adaptability of the same fleet.

For a long period, the Palazzo da Mosto enjoyed another kind of fame – as one of the city's finest hotels. It was known then as the *Leon Bianco* or White Lion and the most illustrious of the city's private visitors stayed there. In 1717 the chronicles mention it as the venue for a duel between two officers of Venice's last great *condottiere*, Count Matthias von der Schulenburg. Duelling between officers must have been common enough; what made this particular episode noteworthy was that each combatant died simultaneously from the other's thrust. Later in the eighteenth century Emperor Joseph II stayed at the *Leon Bianco* and the chroniclers noted that he retired early from several festivities staged in his honour in order to be left in peace at the inn he found so comfortable. Since the fall of the Republic, the history of this ancient house has been obscure, so obscure in fact that it was not until the mid-nineteenth century that the original name of the *Leon Bianco* was discovered and the birthplace of Alvise da Mosto appropriately commemorated with a now all but illegible plaque.

42. Palazzo da Mosto

Palazzo Falier at SS. Apostoli

The Palazzo Falier on the rio di Santissimi Apostoli has undoubtedly changed hands as many times as any other palace in Venice, yet no subsequent owner's name has supplanted that of Falier, one of the most suggestive of early Venetian history and legend. The house has been convincingly dated from the second half of the thirteenth century and could have easily been the *casa domenicale* of the fifty-fifth doge of the Republic, the infamous Marin Falier, who reigned for one year in 1354–5.

The palace is of considerable interest, not only because of its architecture, but also because of its location. It is not on the Grand Canal, but on a minor canal, the rio di SS. Apostoli, which leads almost directly to the ancient market and exchange area of the Rialto. Palazzo Falier is thus part of that group of palaces that make up the surviving examples of the earliest Rialtine settlement. It is built on the same small island and practically adjacent to the Palazzo da Mosto and provides a glimpse, much distorted it is true, of what a corner of Byzantine Venice may have been like. The striking way in which these two closely built houses seem to interlock was a distinctive feature of the city even in those early times. For example, the courtyard of the Palazzo da Mosto can only be reached by passing under the *sottoportego* of the Palazzo Falier, and merchandise arriving by water at the Falier house was unloaded in this same *sottoportego*, which also served as a public passageway for Venetians going from Rialto into the *sestiere* of Cannaregio. The Falier palace with its integral *sottoportego* survives then as an illustration of the way commerce, the waterways, the city's geography, the needs of the populace, and the private property of the patrician class all mingled in a native harmony that was one of the distinctive features of Venice.

The principal safeguard of that egalitarian harmony was the constitution, by which Venetian historians meant the republican government with its elaborate system of checks and balances. In the hall of the Great Council, where the portraits of 76 of the Republic's 120 doges make up the frieze, that of Marin Falier is veiled by a painted black cloth precisely because he attempted to alter the Venetian constitution for his own ends. The story has fascinated many students of Venice's history and none more profoundly than Lord Byron, who wrote, after two years in the city, that the thing that most struck his imagination in Venice was the sight of the black veil. Both he and Swinburne wrote tragedies inspired by the events of the doge's reign, and Donizetti an opera based on Delavigne.

Marin Falier came from one of the most ancient families of Venice. Two

43. Palazzo Falier at SS.
Apostoli

members of the San Vidal branch had been doges in the late eleventh and early twelfth centuries. The branch of SS. Apostoli was extremely rich and Marin held a fief in the marches of Treviso, where he also served as *podestà* and captain, and another fief from the Bishop of Ferrara. He was a friend of Petrarch and represented the Republic as ambassador to Rome. It was in Rome that he was told of his election as doge of Venice. Contemporary accounts remark that though Falier was a proud man, he had done nothing to seek his election. Other chroniclers make much of the fact that, on his return to Venice by ship, foggy weather forced the newly elected doge to come ashore between the columns of the Piazzetta – an extremely evil omen because of the public executions traditionally held there.

The tale of Falier's tragedy can be briefly summarized. At one of the festivities held in the ducal palace a young noble, Michele Steno, was seen to be making a nuisance of himself with the dogaressa's ladies. The doge ordered him away and the young man, in a fit of hot temper, inscribed an insulting verse on the ducal throne. The doge angrily demanded the youth's arrest and Steno was subsequently tried for *lèse-majesté* before the *Quarantia Criminal*. The sentence was confinement for two months to be followed by banishment from Venice for a year. The doge thought Steno should have been hanged or banished for life and took the *Quarantia*'s leniency as an insult to his person and to the dignity of his office. On the same day that Steno was tried and sentenced, the doge received a complaint from the overseer of the Arsenal, who had been physically assaulted by a noble. The overseer's complaint merely strengthened Falier's conviction that the arrogant nobles could insult whom they liked without fear of redress or punishment. According to the chroniclers and the evidence at his trial, Marin Falier now began to conspire with the overseer and with various outraged members of his clan for the overthrow of the patrician government. With the promised support of the *arsenalotti*, the workers in the great shipyards, the coup was to take place on 15 April 1355. One of the conspirators inadvertently gave the game away just a few nights before. He was arrested and under torture confessed the extent of the plot to the horrified officers of the government. In greatest secrecy, the government acted swiftly, forming a special committee to examine the evidence and present their findings to the Council of Ten. On 16 April a number of the chief conspirators were hanged and on the following day the ducal palace was shut and the doge himself was beheaded. The Venetian government had narrowly escaped the fate of numerous other Italian republics where an elected official, a *capitano del popolo*, a *gonfaloniere*, or a *podestà* effected a similar coup and established himself as the founder of a dynasty of princes, marquises, or dukes. The safeguards the Republic introduced after Falier's execution restricted many of the doge's powers and later led to the inaccurate generalization that he was merely a figurehead without influence. But the Venetian constitution, the wonder of Europe, survived another 450 years.

GOTHIC
PALACES

Palazzo Sagredo

The façade of the Palazzo Sagredo on the Grand Canal is a palimpsest of the various stages of Venetian Gothic architecture as deciphered by Ruskin in *The Stones of Venice*. He describes it as 'much defaced, but full of interest'. The left-hand water-gate has the shape of the central part of a late Byzantine arcade and the first-floor windows, with what Ruskin called third-order arch types, link the building to the transitional period between the Veneto-Byzantine and Gothic styles. These windows, which date this part as late thirteenth-century, are too tall, too important, and too early, to be considered merely a mezzanine for the floor above. The fourteenth-century plate tracery of the *piano nobile* is clearly a later addition. But did the later addition replace an earlier upper floor or was it, like so many later enlargements of Byzantine houses, simply added on top of what would have been originally a very small house? Without taking the building to pieces brick by brick, there seems to be no way of knowing for certain. What is clear is that the very top floor and the bulk of the building to the right are indeed later additions. The window-arch types date the right wing to the fifteenth century.

The early ownership of the house is given to the ancient Morosini family and it was not until the beginning of the eighteenth century that a branch of the Sagredo, for centuries resident in the parish of Santa Sofia, bought the palace. It is the interior, now much altered, that reflected their hundred-year tenancy. The original external Gothic staircase had long since disappeared when the Sagredo commissioned Andrea Tirali in 1734 to remodel the stairway built at the back of the *andron*. By removing the barrel-vaulting and eliminating the flights to the upper floors, he created a tall, well-lit stair-hall, which was then frescoed overall with a *Gigantomachia* painted by Pietro Longhi in 1754. The feeling is exuberant Baroque though the fresco was clearly inspired by Giulio Romano's mannerist nightmare, *The Battle of the Giants* in the Palazzo del Tè at Mantua. At the same time, the Sagredo ordered elaborate stucco-work to disguise the beamed ceilings of the Gothic rooms. One room was fitted with a Rococo alcove curtained off by a theatre-like proscenium. A splendid example of the Venetian eighteenth-century bedroom, this ensemble from the Palazzo Sagredo is now on display at the Metropolitan Museum in New York. The Sagredo of Santa Sofia were well-known patrons of the arts, though little or nothing of their painting gallery remains in Venice; four frescoes and a canvas by Gian Battista Tiepolo disappeared in the nineteenth century. Their interest in architecture was not confined to the staircase built by Tirali. In 1753 they had plans drawn up,

44. Palazzo Sagredo seen from the fish market

perhaps by Tommaso Temanza, who was associated with the Sagredo of Santa Ternita, for a new façade for their house at Santa Sofia. It seems that the 'much defaced' façade threatened to collapse into the Grand Canal.

The Sagredo, like other Venetian patrician families, traced their origins to imperial Rome, but instead of discovering there an eponymous clan, they claimed that their name derived from their often being entrusted with state secrets. Their probity led to the governorship of Dalmatia and from there they came to Venice in the ninth century. In the eleventh century Gerardo Sagredo, a Benedictine monk, left Venice to go as a missionary to Hungary, where he became a bishop. He died a martyr, stoned to death outside Buda in 1067. Apart from this saint, the Sagredo also gave to the Church a patriarch of Venice. In the seventeenth century the only Sagredo doge was elected from the branch of Santa Ternita, while the remarkable career of Giovanni is associated with the branch of Santa Sofia. A treasurer and councillor of the Republic at only twenty-seven, he was dispatched as ambassador to Louis XIV to seek French subsidies for the war against the Turk in Crete. Successful in his embassy, he was knighted by the Sun King and permitted to charge the arms of Sagredo di Santa Sofia with the lilies of France. Later he undertook an embassy to Oliver Cromwell and sailed up the Thames with a Venetian flotilla manned by one thousand mariners and displaying over one hundred pieces of artillery. In 1660 he returned again as ambassador to England to assure Charles II of Venice's goodwill toward the restored Stuart monarchy. In addition to his diplomatic career, Giovanni was general in charge of the fortress of Palma and was finally elected a procurator, the life-long appointment second in prestige only to the ducal dignity and arguably a good deal more effective and influential. Agostino Sagredo, the last of this illustrious family, was virulently anti-Austrian and refused every offer of office in the Imperial and Royal government. As a Venetian patriot, however, he filled several offices in the municipal government and was patron of numerous charitable and cultural institutions. He died in London in 1871. His family palace, now mostly rented as office space, was restored by the present owners in 1974.

Palazzo Arian

The mid-fourteenth-century Palazzo Arian in the parish of Sant'Arcangelo Raffaelle is one of the earliest fully Gothic palaces considered in this study. The tracery of the six light *piano nobile* windows is unique in the city. At first glance it appears a lacy arabesque pattern that might have derived from the filigree embellishments of Moorish art, but on closer inspection it is decidedly western in its components. The pattern is made of two rows of interlaced circles with that most Gothic of tracery motifs, the quatrefoil, placed in the centre of each circular unit. The intricacy of it all, and especially the way it fits above and joins the trefoils between the pointed arches of the windows below, can only be understood by examining the joints of the construction. The basic

45. The rich fourteenth-century tracery of Palazzo Arian

module is neither the circle nor the quatrefoil, but the central joint of a group of four of these units. The blackening quality of the pietra d'Istria heightens the delicacy of the expert carving and it is difficult to realize that only the quatrefoil is actually pierced. At the base of four of the six windows there are *plutei* between the columns, two of which, the ones with kneeling figures supporting shields, are old though not of as early a date as the building itself. The appearance of these *plutei* illustrates the continuing influence of the Veneto-Byzantine conventions in palace building of the Gothic period.

46. Palazzo Arian: the first floor windows were remade in the fifteenth century

The palace of the Arian, which today seems remote from the centre of the city, stands on an island that provided refuge for the Roman inhabitants of Padua fleeing from the barbarians. The parish churches in this quarter are of very ancient foundation and it seems that these islands were inhabited by the fishermen of the lagoon, before the mainlanders arrived. The later inhabitants, many of whom were eventually registered as Venetian patricians, probably soon enriched themselves in the river trade that developed between Venice and the towns of the terra-firma. The ancient parishes of Angelo Raffaelle and San Nicolò are those closest to Fusina, the old mouth of the Brenta river and the point from whence the traveller until the early nineteenth century embarked from the mainland to cross the lagoon to Venice.

The Arian family arrived in Venice from Istria and was admitted to the patriciate at the closing of the Great Council in 1297. However, they were excluded from its ranks in the following century for debts of obscure significance. Antonio Arian, the embittered victim of the exclusion, left a will in which he exhorted his sons and daughters never to marry patricians. None the less, one of his sons spent much of his life and vast sums of money attempting to regain for the family its rank and privileges. He contributed especially generously to the Republic's war against the Genoese at Chioggia, but when his largesse failed to procure his re-admission to the *libro d'oro*, the Golden Book of the nobility, he left his wife and family, donned the monastic habit, and went to live in Ferrara. Further attempts were made by members of the family in the fifteenth century, but when the Arian died out in 1650 they were still listed only among the citizens of Venice. The last Arian left the house to his mother's family and for the next hundred years it was in the hands of their descendants. Towards the last years of the Republic, the Pasquaglio family sold it to an ex-nun, Lucia Cicogna, who established a girls' school there and who had her patrician blazon painted over the ancient Arian shields. Lucia died in 1849 and eventually the building became the property of the municipal government, who installed a school in it and who ordered its recently completed restoration.

Palazzo Soranzo

The Palazzo Soranzo in campo San Polo is a fine and relatively pure example of a double Venetian palace. That is to say, it is not simply a palace with a block added at a later date to provide a ballroom or some other extension, such as was the case at the Palazzo Barbaro and the Palazzo Contarini-Corfu, but it is two palaces built at approximately the same time, and thus is close in type to the Giustinian and Mocenigo palaces on the Grand Canal. The left-hand palace is the older of the two, having been built at the end of the fourteenth century and in the first years of the fifteenth. Its twin ground-floor entrances have handsome lintels carved with Byzantine pards, while the paterae and even the shape of the arches on the floor above echo the still strong influence of the Veneto-Byzantine style. The right-hand palace, of the mid-fifteenth century, consciously imitates the earlier building, but the finials atop its bolder Gothic arches clearly identify it as of a later date. The entire double façade is unspoiled by the passion of later centuries for adding projecting balconies at every window and thus destroying the Gothic string course, which here runs the length of both façades.

The façade overlooks the campo San Polo, the largest square in Venice after Saint Mark's, and seems an exception to the Venetian rule that the principal front was on the water. But old prints and maps show that there once was a rio in front of the palace and that its entrances opened onto a *fondamenta*. The outlines of the rio can still be seen in the paving-stones in front of the building. The life of the square is much changed as well: a market was held in San Polo from the thirteenth century and targets were set there for cross-bow practice. In the late fifteenth century, San Bernardino of Siena staged a bonfire of vanities during one of his evangelizing visits to Venice. By 1503 the mood had obviously changed, for shortly after the square had been paved with brick and its well-head erected, a festival was organized here by the boisterous youths of a *compagnia delle calze*, one of the clubs of young nobles who wore the distinctive particoloured hose seen in the paintings of Carpaccio. The festivities included bull-baiting (a favourite Venetian sport), dancing, and fireworks for the populace and for the nobles looking on from their palaces. The Corner, Mocenigo, Bernardo, and Tiepolo all have had family houses overlooking this square.

The Soranzo arrived at San Polo sometime in the mid-fifteenth century, probably after the second palace had been built. Like other great merchant families of the Serenissima, they traced their ancestry to Rome. According to the Soranzo genealogists, their progenitors became the Superanzii of Roman

47. The double palace of Palazzo Soranzo overlooking the campo San Polo

Palazzo Soranzo

Altinum, from whence they migrated to the lagoon. The early Soranzo were among the military tribunes of Byzantine Venice and in 1202 one of them was ranked a captain in the expedition of doge Enrico Dandolo to Zara and Constantinople. The fifty-first doge of the Republic was Giovanni Soranzo, who reigned for sixteen years (1312–28) and who received the Orator of Ravenna, Dante, during his embassy to Venice. Others of the Soranzo are remembered for their military and diplomatic talents. Marino was ambassador to Florence in 1376 as well as captain of the Venetian cavalry in the wars against the della Scala dynasty of Verona. In the fifteenth century, one Vittore was, at separate stages of an illustrious career, both *provveditor* to the armies and generalissimo of the sea. Jacopo Soranzo served as *bailo*, or resident ambassador, to the Sublime Porte in 1644; a kinsman was *bailo* at Corfu and was later made Duke of Candia as Venetian governor of Crete. With all this, the Soranzo had their riches, too. One of them is buried in the nearby church of San Polo with his Venetian nickname as part of his epitaph: 'tocco d'oro', golden touch. The size of their palazzo alone would indicate the wealth of this ancient family, and the Venetian penchant for gilding the lily would have it covered with frescoes by Giorgione as well – but there is no documentary evidence for this decoration. The house is still inhabited by descendants of the Soranzo family.

48. Well-head and early Gothic capital from Palazzo Soranzo at San Polo

Palazzo Falier at San Vidal

The small Gothic Palazzo Falier in the parish of San Vidal is thought to have been constructed in the first half of the fifteenth century. Later on it has been badly altered, especially with the addition of an incongruous upper floor. The two small terraces which extend in front of the house are often mistaken for modern excrescences, but they are, in fact, rare surviving examples of the Venetian *liagò*. One such hip-roofed terrace structure may be seen at the left of Carpaccio's well known *Miracle of the Relic of the Holy Cross* (in the Venice Accademia). This painting is perhaps more familiar for its depiction of the old, wooden Rialto bridge, the gondolas and craft on the canal, and the myriad palaces with their distinctive chimneys, but the Patriarch of Grado's *liagò*, the foundations of which still exist, was the setting of the miracle which gave Carpaccio his subject. It is not quite clear whether the *liagò* was a Gothic innovation or developed from a Veneto-Byzantine prototype.

The antiquity of the Falier's association with the parish, whose church they built in the ninth century, suggests that an older palace must have existed on this site. The fact that many of the Byzantine palaces were not built on the water's edge, but like the Palazzo Falier were set back from it (the Loredan, Farsetti, Barzizza, and Businello palaces, as well as the Fondaco dei Turchi are examples) suggests that the present house may well incorporate the walls of an earlier building; the *liagò* might have developed from Veneto-Byzantine *torreselle*.

The Falier house on the Grand Canal might seem far removed from the ancient centre of the Rialtine islands, but actually it stands directly opposite the mouth of the rio di San Trovaso, the shortest rio cutting through the *sestiere* of Dorsoduro and thus leading to the Giudecca canal, which was the principal artery of Venetian river commerce with the mainland. This ancient link across the canal can be demonstrated in another way: when the parish church on the other side was dedicated, it was to the sons of San Vidal, Saints Gervasio and Protasio, whose name is abbreviated in Venetian as San Trovaso. San Vidal or Vitale was a patron saint of the ancient Falier family which had come to Venice from Fano. Doge Vitale Falier not only erected the parish church, but was credited with rediscovering the body of Saint Mark, whose burial place in the old palatine chapel had been forgotten. The story of the rediscovery is told in the fourteenth-century mosaics of the present basilica. It was this third building of San Marco that Vitale Falier consecrated in 1094. He was succeeded in the dukedom of Venice by his son Ordelafo, whose name appears in contemporary documents in the curious palindrome

Palazzo Falier at San Vidal

Ordelaf Faledro. Ordelafo, one of the great warrior doges of the Republic, sailing as an ally of Baldwin, king of Jerusalem, to conquer Acre, obtained commercial privileges for the Venetians as a result. This expedition not only established the precedent for privileges which were later renewed by the Byzantine emperors, but it also marked one of the earliest acquisitions in what was to be the Venetian commercial empire in the Levant. Ordelafo was also active in the reconquest of Zara in Dalmatia and led his armies to victory in battle against the Paduans. He died a hero's death in 1117 fighting against the Hungarians. The third doge of the Falier family, Marin, lived at SS. Apostoli and the story of his conspiracy belongs to that palace.

In the 1860s one of the mezzanine apartments of the Palazzo Falier was hired by young William Dean Howells, who had come to serve as American consul during the War Between the States. In *Venetian Life* he wrote a charming account of Venice at that period and of his life in the Falier house; there is now a plaque placed on the *calle* wall of the Palazzo to record his stay there.

49. Palazzo Falier at San Vidal: the twin *liagò* project from the *piano nobile*

Palazzo Bernardo

The Palazzo Bernardo on the Grand Canal in the parish of Sant' Aponal was built around the year 1442, and certain details, such as the tracery of the *piano nobile* lateral windows, suggest an affinity with the Ca' d'Oro and therefore with its Venetian architects, Giovanni and Bartolomeo Bon. The specifically Venetian quality of the tracery at the Palazzo Bernardo is particularly evident in the quatrefoil carving of the second *piano nobile*. This imitates, virtually in every detail, the tracery of the loggia of the Doge's Palace. There are the same tiny lion's heads in the triangular spaces between the arches and the same small rosettes in the triangles between the quatrefoils themselves. This tracery motif appears in many fifteenth-century Venetian palaces with the same fidelity to the prototype, which had been introduced over one hundred years earlier.

In many ways the Bernardo house is typical of fifteenth-century architecture; its overall size and shape are reproduced in many later palaces, and its rectangular proportions were to be adopted on differing scales by architects throughout the Renaissance as well. What makes it unique is a peculiar combination of traditional elements. It belongs at once to that group of Gothic palaces where the second *piano nobile* is larger and more important

50. Palazzo Bernardo – detail of the façade showing the quatrefoil tracery of the second *piano nobile*

52. Palazzo Bernardo – the courtyard, well-head and external staircase

than the first (i.e. the Giustinian, Foscari, and Pisani-Moretta palaces) and to the group that can be identified as two-family houses, such as the Soranzo-van Axel and perhaps the original Pisani-Moretta. At the Palazzo Bernardo, the two-family division still exists, with two water-gates leading to separate courtyards, each with an external staircase leading to a different floor of the house. The water-gate on the left leads to a particularly impressive example of this type of courtyard, and the staircase, mounted on large pointed arches, climbs high to the second *piano nobile*.

It is not known for whom this house was built, but by the seventeenth century it was owned by the Bernardo family. These were not the patrician Bernardo whose fine fifteenth-century palace (also called Palazzo Bernardo) stands on the rio di San Polo not far away, but a family of the citizen class who had been merchants dealing in colours and dyes first at the Giudecca and then at the sign of the pumpkin near the fish markets at the Rialto. Various complications over inheritance led to the house being divided up in later generations and finally it had to be auctioned to meet tax payments in the last years of the Republic. By the end of the first decade of the nineteenth century, it was again in the hands of a single owner and by 1840 the whole had been repurchased for the Bernardo family. The house is at present divided into private apartments.

51. Palazzo Bernardo – the façade

Palazzo Loredan degli Ambasciatori

The palace known as the Loredan degli Ambasciatori stands on the Grand Canal in the parish of San Barnaba. Its construction has been dated between 1450 and 1470. It is a building of fine symmetry and balance and is much admired by students of Venetian Gothic architecture, being, like the Palazzo Bernardo, a harmonious and conservative statement of the elements distinctive of the Venetian Gothic palace. It has a fine pointed-arch water-gate surmounted by a finial of the type characteristic of the later fifteenth century. The *portego* of the *piano nobile* is set off from the rest of the façade by the classic quatrefoil tracery adapted from the upper loggia of the ducal palace. The column shafts of the *portego* windows are relatively thick and made of variegated marbles, typical of the traditional colourism of Venetian architecture. But otherwise the façade does not refer much to the conventions of the past. There are no decorative plaques or roundels reflecting Venice's Byzantine legacy. The tracery and corner colonnettes and quoins which frame the façade as they do at the Ca' Foscari are the principal decorative elements along with the pure shapes of the windows themselves. The hint of the transition to follow this period in Venetian Gothic architecture is supplied by the two over-life-size shield-bearing knights placed in tight-fitting scallop-shell niches. One statue leans with a Gothic sway while the other stands firmly planted in a Renaissance *contrapposto* position. Both figures are ascribed to the Lombardesque school of early Renaissance sculpture in Venice and more specifically to the circle of Antonio Rizzo (active 1465–99). Most palaces built in the Gothic style in Venice at this period contain details of the new Lombardesque stamp, but nowhere is this heralding of the Renaissance more gracefully assimilated than in the façade of the Loredan degli Ambasciatori palace.

The branch of the Loredan family which owned the palace at San Barnaba came into prominence in the early eighteenth century with the *provveditor* of Corfu, Antonio Loredan. He and Marshal Matthias von der Schulenburg, the last great *condottiere* of the Republic and the successful reorganizer of the Venetian armies, held out against a massive Turkish invasion of Corfu in 1716. With their resistance, the armies of Schulenburg preserved the Dalmatian coast from invasion and reduced the threat of Turkish raids in the Gulf of Venice. Schulenburg, who stayed with Antonio Loredan in the palace at San Barnaba, was greeted as a hero and a monument was placed in the Arsenal to honour his achievements.

In 1752 Francesco Loredan of the San Barnaba branch was elected the one hundred and sixteenth doge of the Republic. It was he who gave the present sobriquet to his family house. He offered to rent the palazzo to the ambassadors of the Holy Roman Emperor as the seat of their embassy and residence, stipulating that they should hire the building for a minimum of twenty-nine years and pay the rent for that period in advance, and should bear the cost of any repairs. It is not known whether all these terms were accepted, but in 1754 the imperial ambassador, Count Philip Orsini-Rosenburg, took up residence at San Barnaba.

He was succeeded in his embassy by a Genoese count, Giacomo Durazzo, who died in the house a few years before the twenty-nine-year lease expired and only shortly before the collapse of the Republic. In the nineteenth century the house remained in the hands of the Loredan family, but was sold before it was extensively damaged by fire in 1891. After the fire it was restored, giving its façade the slightly new look that it has to this day. The house is privately inhabited.

53. Palazzo Loredan degli Ambasciatori seen through the portico

Ca' d'Oro

The documentation for the palace at Santa Sofia known as the Ca' d'Oro has become almost as rich and complicated as that remarkable building's unique and elaborate façade. The Ca' d'Oro was built for the procurator of San Marco, Marino Contarini, who in 1406 married Sormador Zen and about six years later bought from her family the twelfth-century Veneto-Byzantine palace which once stood on the site. Contarini's decisive role in the construction of the Ca' d'Oro is evident throughout the contemporary documents and may well be taken as a model for the patrician patron's influence in the building of a Venetian palace of the Gothic period. It was obviously Contarini who decided which parts of the old Zen palace were to be incorporated in the new house. His respect for the Veneto-Byzantine building, which is most apparent in the water-gate arcade, is a remarkable illustration of the conservatism, eclecticism, and continuity of Venetian traditions – even more remarkable in such a novel and unique example of

54. Ca' d'Oro seen from the Rialto fish market

55. Ca' d'Oro – the open *portego* tracery and balconies

57. The Bon–Riverti carving and tracery on the Grand Canal façade

56. The courtyard and external staircase of Ca' d'Oro

Flamboyant Gothic architecture and decoration as the Ca' d'Oro. But the innovations are put in perspective by reading Contarini's directives to his builders. At one point, he wanted a corner window of the Palazzo Priuli at San Severo to be copied for its tracery; at another, he specified Rovigno stone for the capitals to be carved like those of the neighbouring Palazzo Sagredo; and very probably he instructed his Milanese and Venetian architects to use the external staircase built for the Porta da Ferro branch of his own family as the model for his own house.

Ca' d'Oro

Contarini's directives do not mean that the builders contributed nothing to the Ca' d'Oro's originality, but there is evidence that even Marco Raverti, the architect of Milan cathedral, who had been in Venice at least a decade before working for Contarini, was willing to adapt his style to the exigencies of his patron and to Venetian architectural tradition and conventions. His hand and those of the numerous members of his Lombard workshop have been identified in the building, but mostly in details such as the double cable moulding of the corners or the carving of the first-floor tracery. Contarini contracted Raverti from the very beginning in 1425; only later did the Venetian workshop of Giovanni and Bartolomeo Bon collaborate – and quarrel – with the Lombard stonecutters.

58. The early fifteenth-century façade of Ca' d'Oro

For all its exceptional qualities, the Ca' d'Oro is very much a Venetian house of a traditional type. The *portego* and water-gate sections of the flat façade have arcades, reminiscent in their openness of the Veneto-Byzantine *curia* – and on the ground floor, at least, directly derived from a building of that style and period. The right-hand section of the façade, masking the lateral living rooms, could be described as a *torresella*; the vertically disposed wall space easily suggests such a tower. It was long thought that a corresponding *torresella* wing was intended for the left side as well, but such an hypothesis ignores the internal symmetry of the present building.

The most striking contribution of the Ca' d'Oro façade to the vocabulary of fifteenth-century Venetian Gothic architecture is certainly the tracery. That of the *piano nobile portego* is particularly fine, a refined elaboration of the tracery found at the ducal palace, and the upper-floor tracery could have been based on motifs taken from the windows on the rio side of the ducal palace. In both cases, the tracery is more delicately carved and the treatment more sensitive than that of its prototypes, though something of the vigour of the original has been sacrificed. The tracery of the single windows on either side of the *portego* was derived from the Palazzo Priuli; it reappears later at the Palazzo Giustinian and the Palazzo Bernardo.

The richness of the marble facing and the intricacy of the decoration, whether taken from the Zen palace or carved anew, must have been even more impressive in Contarini's day. In 1431, he commissioned one Zuane da Franza to pick out the carving in ultramarine and red and to gild generously other details. It is from this latter embellishment that the house took its popular name, the Ca' d'Oro, or golden house. As was traditional in Venice, the land side was less elaborate, though the standard of decoration is very high. A magnificent finial-topped gateway arch leads to the courtyard, where the centre-piece is the highly carved well-head signed by the Bon. The *piano nobile* is reached by an extremely rich external staircase with decorated treads, probably built by Raverti. The plan is typically Venetian with the central *portego* ending in an L-branch at the water. The present restorations are uncovering the original round-arched doors of the interior rooms and an early, light-coloured *terrazzo* floor.

The Contarini owned the Ca' d'Oro for only two generations. A marriage

Ca' d'Oro

of Marino's granddaughter to Pietro Marcello in 1484 brought it into the ancient Marcello family, and in 1620 part of the house passed to a branch of the Loredan, again through marriage. In the last years of the Republic, the divided house was rented by the Bressa family. After the fall of Venice, it changed hands many times. In 1840 it was bought by Prince Alexander Trubetskoy for the ballerina Maria Taglioni. The story is told that young Trubetskoy had pleaded with her to intercede with the Czar of Russia for the release of his father from Siberian exile. She granted his request and was rewarded by her youthful admirer, and perhaps lover, with the gift of the golden house. Whatever the truth, it was at this period that the architect G. B. Meduna was called in to consolidate the building and to redecorate it to the dancer's taste. Whoever was responsible, Meduna's restoration resulted in the demolition and dispersal of the famous external staircase. The present one is a reconstruction using old materials patiently collected by Baron Giorgio Franchetti, who bought the house in 1894. Franchetti spent enormous sums and many years restoring the house to his own particular criteria. Though he lived in it, he neither thought of furnishing it as a house nor did he attempt an historically exact reconstruction. He consulted his own taste as an aesthete and collector and he wanted the Ca' d'Oro to become, along with his collections, a unified work of art in itself. With a statement of his intentions, he bequeathed the house to the municipality of Venice and retired to the mezzanine of the adjoining Palazzo Fontana, where he died in 1922. Since the opening of the house as a museum in 1927 it has provided a unique setting for Franchetti's remarkable collections. At present it is being restored.

60. The Veneto-Byzantine water entrance and the Gothic balcony brackets

59. Ca' d'Oro – a view of the first floor and of the Grand Canal

61. OVERLEAF LEFT The Gothic Palazzo Contarini–Corfu with (left) Scamozzi's addition, the Palazzo Contarini degli Scrigni

62. OVERLEAF RIGHT The courtyard of Palazzo Barbaro

Palazzo Barbaro

The Palazzo Barbaro at Santo Stefano is one of the most interesting of fifteenth-century Venetian palaces, not only for its architecture and the alterations made to it, but also for the story of its patrician owners during the days of the Republic and its role in the literary and artistic life of the nineteenth century. The Barbaro house is actually two palaces. The Gothic building can be dated 1425 from an item in the accounts of the Ca' d'Oro when the Venetian stonecutter Giovanni Bon had his wages docked because he had left the building at Santa Sofia to work for the Barbaro at Santo Stefano. The second part of the Palazzo Barbaro is the wing added by Antonio Gaspari in 1694–8 to house a ballroom at the level of the second *piano nobile*.

On the evidence of the external staircase leading to the *piano nobile*, there seems little doubt that the Palazzo Barbaro incorporates remains of an earlier building, though what the original house was like is impossible to determine. For the rest, the Gothic façade and the interior plan are typical of the period in which the Bon family worked. Compared with the Ca' d'Oro, the Palazzo Barbaro is obviously conservative. The thick-leafed capitals with cherub's heads are a typical Bon motif, but otherwise the Venetian builders attempted little elaboration on a scale like that of the Ca' d'Oro. Even the classic quatrefoil tracery, adapted from the Doge's Palace for the *piano nobile*, seems surprisingly tentative since it is unpierced. The most elaborate carvings on the Gothic façade are the brackets that support the balcony of the first floor, one of the few authentic fifteenth-century balconies left in the city. The Gothic water-gate on the left of the façade now leads to the second courtyard, where there is a steep external staircase to the second *piano nobile*. Originally this archway and the arcade along the rio were part of a *sottoportego* like that of the Falier palace at SS. Apostoli.

Late in the fifteenth century, the Gothic façade was given decorative touches which point to the arrival of the Lombardesque or early Renaissance taste in Venice. The small plaques between the *portego* and lateral windows on both principal floors are in the Lombardesque style as is the central water-gate with its fluted pilasters and portrait-bust medallions of the emperor Octavian and of Marcus Agrippa in the spandrels. But the most significant alteration to both plan and elevation came in the seventeenth century with the addition of Gaspari's wing. The second *piano nobile* became the principal floor because not only Gaspari's handsome ballroom was on that level, but also heavy balconies, built across the width of both façades. The house underwent extensive

63. The Gothic Palazzo Barbaro with its seventeenth-century addition

64. OVERLEAF LEFT The ballroom of Palazzo Barbaro

65. OVERLEAF RIGHT The enfilade of rooms on the second *piano nobile* of Palazzo Barbaro

remodelling and redecoration at this time and in the early eighteenth century. A fine Venetian library room with lacquer-work bookcases was installed in the top floor of the Gothic building. The dining room, also in the Gothic part of the house, has a splendid *terrazzo* floor inlaid with mother of pearl and a motif of flowers and ribbons, and a ceiling painted by Gian Battista Tiepolo. But the most elaborate decoration was reserved for the stuccoed ballroom.

The Barbaro of Santo Stefano traced their descent from Roman consular nobility established near Trieste and later at Eraclea. Their arms, which figure repeatedly along with military trophies and the double-headed imperial eagle in the stucco decoration of the ballroom, are *argent*, a *circlet gules* representing the bloodied turban-cloth of a Saracen taken in the First Crusade. In the late fifteenth century the Barbaro, distinguished by riches and the military prowess of their ancestors, served the Republic in various important embassies. The most illustrious of the family were undoubtedly the brothers, Daniele and Marc'Antonio. Daniele was a humanist, collector, ambassador to England, active at the Council of Trent, and finally, Patriarch of Aquileia; Marc'Antonio was a Senator and ambassador to France, and with his brother commissioned Palladio, Veronese and Alessandro Vittoria in 1560 to design the famous Villa Barbaro at Maser. In the seventeenth century, Antonio Barbaro revived the family's military traditions at the battle of the Dardanelles and fought in Crete, Dalmatia, and Albania. He also provided the church of Santa Maria del Giglio with its extraordinary Baroque façade by Giuseppe Sardi, extolling in sculpture not the saints of the church, but the merits of the Barbaro family.

Today the house is more often associated with its guests than with the Barbaro family. This tradition may be said to have begun with the long visit of that extraordinary patroness of Renaissance art, Isabella d'Este, marchioness of Mantua. But the guests of Mr and Mrs Daniel Curtis of Boston, who bought the upper two floors of the house in 1882, are perhaps the best remembered. It was in their apartments that Henry James and John Singer Sargent came to stay; Robert Browning gave readings in the eighteenth-century library and the octogenarian Monet here painted his magical evocations of glimmering Venetian façades. The ballroom, with its great canvases by Piazzetta and Sebastiano Ricci, is particularly linked with the Curtises and their guests, as it was in this setting that Sargent painted the group portrait of the Curtis family which now hangs in the Royal Academy. They frequently let their *piano nobile* to friends when they were away, and after a summer's stay, the eccentric Mrs Jack Gardner of Boston was inspired to build her Boston townhouse, now the Fenway Court Museum, using the Barbaro as a model. Another summer tenant, though this time fictional, was described by Henry James in *The Wings of a Dove*. During one of his long visits, James wrote *The Aspern Papers* at a Venetian lacquer *trumeau* still to be seen in the palace. In *The Wings of a Dove* he wrote of the ballroom at the Palazzo Barbaro: 'The warmth of the southern summer was still in the high, florid rooms, palatial chambers where hard, cool pavements took reflections in

66. Palazzo Barbaro on the Grand Canal, seen from the Palazzo Contarini-Polignac

67. OVERLEAF LEFT The Gothic land entrance and rio façade of Palazzo Soranzo-van Axel

68. OVERLEAF RIGHT Palazzo Foscari with (left) the Giustinian palaces

their lifelong polish, and where the sun on the stirred sea-water, flickering up through open windows, played over the painted "subjects" in the splendid ceilings – medallions of purple and brown, of brave old melancholy colour, medals as of old reddened gold, embossed and beribboned, all toned with time and all flourished and scolloped and gilded about, set in their great moulded and figured concavity (a nest of white cherubs, friendly creatures of the air), and appreciated by the aid of that second tier of smaller lights, straight openings to the front, which did everything . . . to make of the place an apartment of state.'

Palazzo Giustinian at San Barnaba

The double palace of the Giustiniani and the great Palazzo Foscari together make up the great show-piece of fifteenth-century Gothic architecture on the Grand Canal. In fact, so often are these palaces considered a unit, and so often do the ancient documents speak of three Giustiniani houses, that a considerable confusion has arisen. Recent archival research has shown that the first of the three palaces owned by the Giustiniani no longer exists, nor was it incorporated into the fabric of the present Palazzo Foscari. It was built on property acquired by Nicolò and Giovanni Giustiniani in the mid-fifteenth century and stood on a site now partly occupied by the courtyard of Ca' Foscari and would have overlooked what is now the rio nuovo. The Giustiniani sold this first of their houses to the Foscari, who had it pulled down. The other two palaces, which still exist on the Grand Canal, were probably begun about 1452.

The Giustinian palace is a superb example of that peculiarly Venetian phenomenon, the double palace, though the two parts are not as closely joined as they are at the Soranzo house at San Polo or even at the later double Mocenigo house at San Samuel. From behind the two Giustiniani houses it is evident that the round-arched central water-gate of the Grand Canal façade and the single windows on each floor above it are not really part of either of the two blocks, but belong to a passageway only one room deep, connecting the two houses. None the less, this link wall is an integral part of the double façade and at the *piano nobile* level is flanked by single windows with elaborate tracery, which call attention to its aesthetic function as the central and vertical axis of an otherwise extremely long, horizontal façade. Without the link wall, its large water-gate, and the elaborate tracery windows, the whole would break into two handsome, but rather repetitious units with the focus on the *portego* window groups of each separate house.

In both cases, it is the *portego* tracery that reveals the authorship of the building; it is most certainly by Bartolomeo Bon, author of the *Porta della Carta* at the ducal palace. That two Giustinian brothers commissioned these separate yet connected houses is a reminder that most Venetian palaces were single family units and that brothers frequently built separate houses which then became, in the special Venetian sense, seats of separate branches of the family. Here one branch became known as the Giustinian dei Vescovi, of the Bishops, and the other as the Giustinian dalle Zogie, of the Jewels. At various times in the history of the Republic at least fifteen palaces have been designated Giustinian.

69. The double palace of the Giustinian family, built by Bartolomeo Bon

71. The Giustinian and Foscari palaces – a general view

70. The fifteenth-century Palazzo Foscari at the volta del canal

The Giustiniani were an ancient and illustrious patrician family and two of the city's more picturesque legends are associated with them. The first, of course, concerns their origins. Justin, emperor of Byzantium, nephew and son-in-law of the great Justinian, had a grandson, Justinian, who left Constantinople in 670 for Istria, where he gave his name to Justinopolis (now Capodistria in Jugoslavia). From there his descendants arrived on the lagoon, settling first at Malamocco on the lido, and later, with the transfer of the government to the Rialtine islands, in Venice itself. In the twelfth century this family of imperial descent was threatened with extinction, all the young male issue having perished, according to the legend, in battle against the Byzantine emperor, Emmanuel Comnenus. There remained only one young Giustinian who might save the family, but he was in religious orders and a monk at San Nicolò del Lido. In recognition of the Giustiniani's valour, service to the state, and extensive patrimony, members of the great Morosini and Falier families pleaded with Pope Alexander III to release young Nicolò from his vows and permit him to marry. The pope acquiesced and Nicolò was married in great state to Anna, daughter of the doge Vitale Falier II, bringing with her a dowry of three *contrade* (streets) of houses in the parishes of San Giovanni in Bragora, San Moisè, and San Pantaleon. The couple fulfilled their service to the state and to the Giustinian family with a progeny of nine sons and three daughters. Their descendants still exist in Italy and the last Giustinian to live in Venice died as recently as 1962. Having saved the family from extinction, Nicolò retired to the contemplative life of his monastery and his wife followed his pious example, taking the veil in the convent she founded, Sant' Adriano di Costanziaco, known in the dialect as Sant'Arrian and used today as the ossuary for the bones disinterred from Venice's cemetery island.

Numerous illustrious Giustiniani, such as the first Patriarch of Venice, Saint Lorenzo Giustinian, are associated with other of the family's many palaces, but it was in this house that Marcantonio, their only doge (1684–8), was born. Under his reign, Venice's great *capitan da mar*, Francesco Morosini, brought the whole of the Morea (Peloponnese) back into the Venetian domain, conquering Athens and gravely damaging the Parthenon, enslaving or killing more than 200,000 of Mohammed IV's Turkish subjects, and thus giving the dying Republic her last real taste of victory over the infidel enemy.

After the fall of the Republic, the Palazzo Giustinian passed into the hands of the painter, Natale Schiavone, who housed her important collection of old masters there. But the best known of the palace's inhabitants was Richard Wagner, who arrived in 1858 for a seven months' stay. After having the rooms of his apartment hung in dark red and installing the Erard grand piano rescued from his Swiss creditors, Wagner settled down to work on the composition of *Tristan und Isolde*. While living in the Palazzo Giustinian, he studied Schopenhauer and the teachings of Buddha, broke off his work for a daily gondola ride to the Piazza and, according to his Venetian notebook, flirted with the idea of suicide. Nevertheless, he managed to complete the second act of the opera and to prepare himself for his work on *Parsifal*. Venice was always an inspiration to him and he returned often. His death in the city twenty-five years after his stay in the Palazzo Giustinian became as much a part of Venice's story as were the legends of the house itself.

Palazzo Foscari

The great fifteenth-century palace of the Foscari dominates, with the later Palazzo Balbi, the sharp bend in the Grand Canal between the Rialto and San Marco, known to Venetians as the *volta del canal*. In its day, the Palazzo Foscari must have seemed the most imposing of the new palaces and in many ways it could be taken to represent the confident might and riches of the Venetian state at the moment before the Portuguese discovered their trade route to the East, before Constantinople fell to the Turks, and before Venetian mainland ambition and expansion received the paralysing check dealt them by the League of Cambrai. It was also, both in its day and still today, more than any other building in Venice, the monument to the talent, ambition, and downfall of a single individual, Doge Francesco Foscari.

The site originally belonged to the Giustinian family who had built a house further back from the Grand Canal on the rio di San Pantaleon (now the rio nuovo). In about 1430 the Giustinian house was purchased by the Senate and given to the Republic's ally and *condottiere*, Gianfrancesco Gonzaga, lord and captain of Mantua. Towards the middle of the century it was bought by Doge Francesco Foscari, who had it torn down and who employed Bartolomeo Bon to begin work on the great house we see today. Foscari's wealth was certainly equalled by that of many of his patrician colleagues, but his talents, his temperament, and his strong personality marked him as a man apart. By the time he reached the ducal dignity in 1423, his accomplishments made him a target of jealousy and intrigue. At the age of twenty-seven he became a senator, at thirty-one he held the high magisterial office of Avogador of the Republic, and by the time he was forty-five he was elected a procurator of San Marco. Four years later he was elected doge, but only after a fierce electoral battle with Pietro Loredan had prolonged the complicated procedure by ten further scrutinies. From the date of his election and for the thirty-four years that he reigned, he became the victim of an unrelenting vendetta by the Loredan and their kinsmen, the Donà and the Barbarigo.

Besides the clique set against him, one other voice spoke out against Foscari with such authority as to blind historians to his claim to be judged fairly in the eyes of posterity. The octogenarian doge, Tommaso Mocenigo, realizing that his life was drawing to a close, drew up what might be called a Farewell Address to the Republic, still regarded as one of the most remarkable documents of the Venetian quattrocento. In it Mocenigo described the economic position of Venice, meticulously enumerating the numbers of her merchant fleet and the financial returns on their voyages: in short, the balance sheet of the flourishing fifteenth-century republic. Fascinating as Mocenigo's figures are, they were drawn up for political ends. The old doge, referring to the election that would ensue on his death, concluded, 'Why some say that they wish to elect Messer Francesco Foscari I do not know, for said Ser Francesco Foscari spreads lies and other statements without foundation and swoops and soars more than a hawk or falcon. And if you make him doge, which God forbid, you will shortly be at war. . . .'. Mocenigo goes on to point out that Venice's economy would be ruined by Foscari's policies of war and expansion. Foscari's election was followed by prolonged warfare on the mainland and there is no doubt that this involvement with the politics of the terra-firma was, in the long run, detrimental to Venice's fortunes. But the policy of mainland conquest and expansion had, in fact, begun under Mocenigo and his predecessor, and Foscari was virtually forced to defend Venetian territory against the encroachment and ambitions of the Visconti dynasty of Milan.

72. The Grand Canal looking from Palazzo Foscari at the volta del canal to Ca' Rezzonico

The personal attack on Foscari by the Loredan clique centred at first on his son Jacopo. In 1444–5 charges of political corruption, insinuating the doge's involvement, were brought against the young man and he was sentenced to banishment from Venice for a year. Next, Jacopo was accused of murder by one of the clique, the same member of the Donà family who had instigated the first charges. Punishment by exile was again the sentence. Finally, in 1456, Jacopo was accused of treason. Loredan demanded that he should be beheaded, but the courts found evidence only of reckless talk and not treason, and voted to prolong Jacopo's exile. The baseless legend grew up around the treason trial that the doge had been forced to witness the torture of his son. But even the currency of such a rumour illustrates the tragic proportions that the persecution of Foscari began to assume in the eyes of his contemporaries.

The implacable Loredan and his allies manipulated the Council of Ten to humiliate the doge at every turn. In 1457, Jacopo Loredan, Girolamo Donà, and Girolamo Barbarigo, as officers of this powerful government council, which at times could assume the virtually unlimited powers of a committee of public safety, demanded that he should be removed from office on the trumped-up grounds of his physical incapacity. Before their motion could be presented to the Maggior Consiglio and the unconstitutional nature of the entire procedure exposed, the Council of Ten forced Foscari's resignation. He returned as a private citizen to his palace on the *volta del canal* and died a broken man shortly afterwards. The entire tragedy assumed the proportions of a serious crisis in Venetian internal politics and resulted in future vigilance over the Council of Ten's powers. Specific legal provision was made that the ducal office was to be held for life. While the Loredan faction was too powerful to be publicly reprimanded, the magnificence of Foscari's state funeral and the orations recited somewhat redressed the balance. Byron made these events the subject of his tragedy *The Two Foscari*, which was later adapted for the libretto of Verdi's opera of the same title.

In 1574 the Palazzo Foscari was again a centre of attention. Henry of Valois,

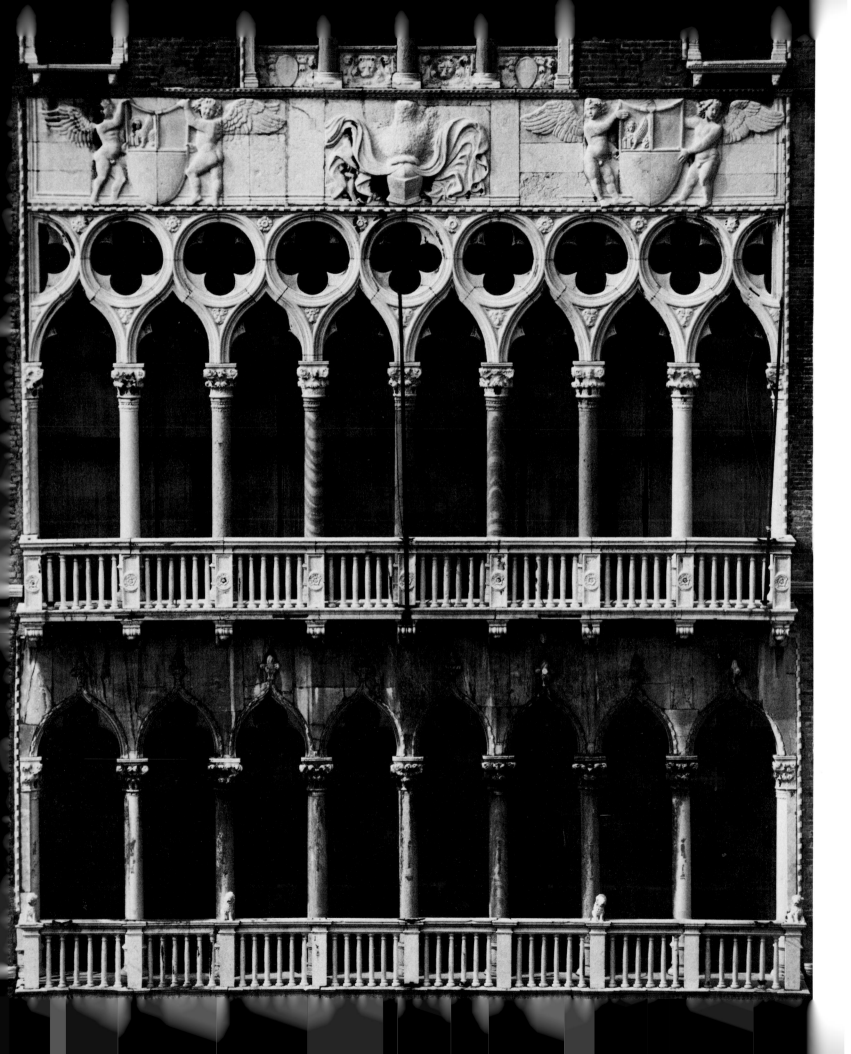

fleeing from his thankless role as elective king of Poland, arrived in Venice on his way to France to be crowned as King Henry III. He spent seven nights in the Palazzo Foscari at the expense of the Republic in the bedroom next to that in which Francesco Foscari had died. Not since the legendary visit of the Emperor Frederick Barbarossa and the Pope Alexander III had a state visit so gripped the imagination of the Venetians. The young king was fêted on a spectacular scale and the artistic riches of the Republic were laid at his feet: quite literally, in fact, since the floor of his bedroom was of Venetian mosaic work executed from designs by Paolo Veronese. A portrait of Henry was commissioned from Titian and hung in the bedroom in a frame designed and carved by Alessandro Vittoria. The caryatids of the great fireplace were also carved by Vittoria and the walls were covered with gilded stamped leather from the state manufactory. Palladio was commissioned to build a plaster archway at the lido that is commemorated in many of the paintings depicting the king's arrival in the city. Venetians have never ceased to recall the great banquet given to him, where the plates, place settings, glasses, and elaborate statuary centre-pieces were designed by Sansovino – and all made in sugar. On the morning of the great banquet in the sala del Maggior Consiglio, the young king was taken to the Arsenal to inspect the keel of a ship that had just been laid; that same afternoon he returned to see the very same ship, completed in every detail, sail fully manned from the docks. Henry is said never to have recovered from the impression made on him by the wonders, prodigies, and wealth of the Republic. In the eighteenth century, the Palazzo Foscari was again fitted up for the visit of a sovereign, Frederick IV of Denmark. The best-known souvenir of this state visit is the famous painting by Luca Carlevaris of the regatta staged in his honour.

Later in the same century the house was enlarged at the back, thus diminishing the impressive courtyard with its two well-heads and causing the disappearance of the Gothic external staircase. From that time on, with the decline of the Republic's fortunes, the Palazzo Foscari began to suffer neglect. In the nineteenth century the municipality bought it for 40,000 lire and restored it to house technical schools established in honour of a visit by the Austrian emperor, Ferdinand I. Successive restorations in the nineteenth century and its present role as part of the recently chartered University of Venice have virtually erased all trace of its former magnificence, but its position on the Grand Canal, its handsome fifteenth-century façade with rich tracery, precious marble columns, and the huge putti-supported arms of the Foscari, still evoke its former part in the life and history of the Republic.

73. The variegated marble columns, fifteenth-century quatrefoil tracery and heraldic frieze of Palazzo Foscari

Palazzo Soranzo-van Axel

The late fifteenth-century Gothic Palazzo Soranzo-van Axel is a good illustration of an important house built on a small canal in the city's interior. The Veneto-Byzantine house of the Gradenigo family, which stood here originally, probably conformed as much to the irregular site as the present Gothic building does. Palazzo Soranzo-van Axel has two waterfront or principal façades corresponding to the two canals that intersect outside it. For the tourist on foot, the house may seem buried in the centre of a confusing labyrinth, but should he come from the north of the city by boat, as did all the river traffic from Germany, the rio della Panada would lead him straight to the palace. And any of the three small canals opening onto the Grand Canal opposite the Rialto market also lead almost directly to the Palazzo Soranzo.

The patrician Gradenigo family came first to the lagoon city of Aquileia from Transylvania. On the destruction of Aquileia by Attila in 452, they fled to a more easily defensible peninsula where, according to tradition, they founded the patriarchal city of Grado. They became established in Venice in later centuries; one of their three doges presided over the epochal closing of the Great Council of 1297. A branch of the Gradenigo lived in what was then the parish of San Canciano until 1473, when they sold their ancient family house to Nicolò Soranzo, a procurator of San Marco, for 4,000 gold ducats. He rebuilt the palace in late Gothic style, allowing elements of the original building to be used in the decoration, as did Marino Contarini at the Ca' d'Oro. The carved frieze in the larger courtyard is clearly Veneto-Byzantine and some of the arch openings probably echo or incorporate similar openings in the original building.

Although the site of the palace makes its plan somewhat unusual, two courtyards were once common to many Venetian Gothic palaces. Palazzo Soranzo-van Axel is interesting in that its double courtyards escaped spoliation when the fashion for internal staircases and the enlargement of palaces on the land side became common. In the larger courtyard the stairway rises in two flights to the second *piano nobile*, whereas in the smaller it reaches only the first principal floor. Such an arrangement implies separate apartments for two units of the same family branch, but there is little documentary evidence for such a clear-cut division. This kind of functional division can only be deduced from the separateness of the two staircase courtyards and by contrasting such a building with other Gothic palaces of the same period where the first and second floors were connected by a secondary internal wooden staircase. Unfortunately, few such internal wooden staircases survive

74. Palazzo Soranzo-van Axel – a general view from the canal bridge

Palazzo Soranzo-van Axel

from the Gothic period and none in the double-courtyard houses. Besides the two splendid and picturesque external staircases, the first courtyard has an elaborately carved *vera da pozzo*, or well-head, of Verona marble, a traditional and obviously functional fixture. The one at the Palazzo Soranzo shows the derivation of these well-heads from the Gothic capital; it has large fully carved acanthus leaves at its angles and in the space between, where rosettes generally appeared on the capital, the sculptor has carved vases with elaborate bouquets. The *fondamenta* entrance to the larger courtyard still has its original fifteenth-century carved-larchwood door with a *bataor*, or knocker, in the form of a fish.

75. The courtyard, well-head and external staircase of the Palazzo Soranzo-van Axel

The canalside quay onto which this doorway opens was once known as the *fondamenta* Sanudo, the name of the second family associated with the palace. A branch of the Sanudo lived here in the sixteenth and seventeenth centuries. The nineteenth doge of Venice introduced the name Sanuto for his family, meaning, it is supposed, 'prudently sane or wise' (*sennato* in modern Italian). The earlier family name was Candiano and was borne by no fewer than five doges before the year 1000. This ancient patrician family claimed descent from the illustrious *gens* Livia, who counted among their members numerous tribunes, consuls, pontifices maximi, and four empresses, as well as the famous historian Livy, who was born in Patavium (modern Padua) in 59BC. Sixteen hundred years after Livy had begun his history of Rome, a Venetian descendant of his family, Marin Sanudo, began the monumental fifty-eight volumes of diaries, which are still considered an invaluable source of sixteenth-century Italian and Venetian history. Marin Sanudo's branch of the family lived near San Giacomo dell'Orio, but no one writing about the life of Venice, her patricians or her palaces, could neglect to mention his name – if only in passing.

From the Sanudo, the house returned briefly to a branch of the Soranzo family until in 1652 it was sold to the van Axel, whose descendants lived in the palace until 1920. The van Axel were a Flemish merchant family from near Malines in Brabant. They and the Widman from Carinthia were among the few non-Italian families admitted to the Venetian patriciate in the mid-seventeenth century. Such aggregations were not uncommon at this period, owing to the increasing exhaustion of Venetian resources, the heavy expense of the wars against the Turk, and the willing generosity, for the price of ennoblement, of the recently enriched merchants of the city. The van Axel maintained the palace in a style consonant with their newly acquired dignity and inserted their arms in the Gothic spandrel of their land entrance; they further consolidated their position with marriages into the Balbi, Bembo, and Foscarini families. At present, the Palazzo Soranzo-van Axel is divided into apartments, several of which are let as offices.

Palazzo Contarini-Fasan

The tiny Palazzo Contarini-Fasan in the parish of San Moisè was built in the middle of the fifteenth century, though its remarkably picturesque qualities led early critics to date it from as early as the thirteenth century. For Venice, it is an architecturally unique building, being only one room wide and therefore hardly a palace at all. But the rich decoration of its façade is also unique in Venice and it is for that reason that it is included with grander and more traditional types of Venetian domestic architecture. The alternating Istrian stone quoins and the richly carved cable moulding colonnettes that frame each floor of the narrow façade suggest that the building is complete as we see it. Jacopo de'Barbari's map of 1500 indicates that there was a pointed-arch water-gate opening onto the Grand Canal and this helps make sense of an otherwise extremely curious arrangement. The water-gate was blocked up

77. Palazzo Contarini-Fasan, mid-fifteenth-century Gothic. It is known locally as the house of Desdemona

76. A view of the palaces opposite the Salute: the Contarini-Fasan is third from left

Palazzo Contarini-Fasan

when the house became a part of the adjacent Venier–Contarini house, but the difference in the façades and elevations makes it obvious that the two houses were originally quite separate units. Ruskin gives the architect of the Contarini-Fasan credit for having built a house to fit an extremely narrow site and the earliest views of the city would seem to support his assessment. The most noteworthy features of the house, apart from its diminutive size, are the balconies, which represent the only appearance of wheel tracery in Venetian Gothic balconies. Possibly they were carved by members of the Raverti workshop since the patterns can be related to the eastern apse window tracery of Milan cathedral.

Though little is known of the history of the palace, it has always captured the fancy of the Venetians and has long been popularly known as the house of Desdemona. A patrician lady named Disdemona did live in Venice, and according to the chronicles, and later popular recounting of her story, she was murdered by her jealous husband, a member of the Moro family, but long before the Palazzo Contarini-Fasan was built. Shakespeare knew a version of the tale from Giovanni Battista Giraldi's collection of Italian stories, the *Hecatommithi*, first printed in 1565. In writing *Othello*, Shakespeare followed Giraldi in many details. However, the villainous subtlety of Iago was very much his own creation and, convincing as his depiction of Venetians, Venice, and Cyprus may seem, his transformation of a member of the Moro family into a Moorish general of the Republic would have been incomprehensible to the Venetians of the day.

The designation of the palace as the Palazzo Contarini-Fasan is as obscure in origin as is the supposed connection with Shakespeare's heroine. The name Fasan is supposed to derive from the passion of a former owner for pheasant shooting, a reminder that branches of patrician families and their palaces were often distinguished by curious sobriquets.

Palazzo Pisani-Moretta

The Palazzo Pisani-Moretta in the parish of San Tomà on the Grand Canal belonged to one of the many branches of the Pisani family. The branch which lived at San Fantin produced the great naval hero of the fourteenth century, Vettor Pisani, but was extinct by the seventeenth century. The Pisani of Santa Maria del Giglio and Santo Stefano were renowned for their vast banking fortune and are frequently referred to in Venetian documents as the Pisani del Banco. The name Moretta attached to the San Tomà branch is perhaps a corruption of Almorò, the name of the first of the Pisani to settle in this parish in about 1420.

The late fifteenth-century façade of the palace displays noteworthy examples of Venetian Gothic tracery. At the first *piano nobile* there is the quatrefoil tracery derived from the ducal palace and common, in its most straightforward form, to such fifteenth-century palaces as the Foscari, Giustinian, Loredan degli Ambasciatori, Contarini-Corfu, and Bernardo; the second *piano nobile* tracery is of the less usual, intersecting semicircle type found again at the Giovanelli and Cavalli palaces. Palazzo Pisani-Moretta is also an example of the Gothic palace with two *piani nobili*, the second and higher of which is the more important. Of the palaces mentioned above, only the Foscari and Giustinian share this type of elevation. Of all these Gothic houses, the Pisani-Moretta is one of the latest, having been built in the 1470s.

However, there has always been some confusion as to the date of this house, because of the work that was done on the façade in the sixteenth century. The corner pilasters are of the later period, as are the ovolo and dentil string-courses, but the balconies are arguably original. The colonnettes of the balconies, which were widely copied, are probably derived from a Tuscan model such as the base of Donatello's *Judith and Holofernes* (1460) and are part of the original construction. The collection of paintings formed in the sixteenth century was long the principal fame of the house. There were works by Palma Vecchio and the two Bellini, portraits by Tintoretto, and the splendid canvas of *The Family of Darius at the Feet of Alexander* by Paolo Veronese. When a radical redecoration of the house was undertaken in the eighteenth century, the fame of this picture was such that the Pisani commissioned a companion piece from Piazzetta, *The Death of Darius*, which can still be seen in Venice at the Ca' Rezzonico. The famous Veronese was sold to the National Gallery in London in 1857 by the executors and heirs of the last Pisani of San Tomà for £13,560.

The eighteenth-century redecoration was undertaken at great expense by

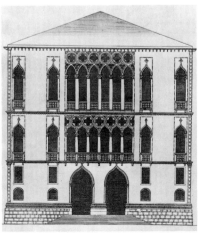

78. An engraving of Palazzo Pisani-Moretta (Cicognara, British Museum)

Palazzo Pisani-Moretta

the forceful Chiara Pisani-Moretta, who spent twenty-five years in litigation trying to prove that her brother Pietro was illegitimate. Had she succeeded she could have carried out her ambitious programme with his portion of the family patrimony as well. As it is, the work she began in 1742 resulted in a significant re-arrangement of the interior. Three features of her project are particularly noteworthy. The most obvious from the outside, and perhaps the most dubious in taste, is the large terrace balustrade she strung across the roof line. Jutting out on scrolled brackets, it weighs down on and seems to squash the handsome quatrefoil tracery below. The attics behind the terrace were converted into a series of Rococo stuccoed apartments. The attic floor was to be reached by the uppermost flights of an extremely grand staircase Chiara had installed. To construct it, the old external staircase and part of the

79. The Grand Canal with (from left to right) Palazzo Tiepolo, Palazzo Pisani-Moretta, Palazzo Barbarigo della Terrazza and Palazzo Capello-Layard

courtyard were demolished and a section of the *portego* on each *piano nobile* was sacrificed. In plan, the staircase is something like Tirali's invention for the Palazzo Sagredo at Santa Sofia. It begins in two flights and returns in one, though Tirali's only reached the first floor, whereas Chiara's massive, column-supported affair rose through all three floors to the top of the house. On the *piano nobile* she had the *portego* transformed into a marvel of Murano looking-glasses, wall-sconces, and chandeliers all set in *marmorino,* Rococo stucco decoration and more mirrors. A ceiling was commissioned from Gian Battista Tiepolo and the great Veronese was hung with its pendant by Piazzetta in a side room.

The *portego* is to this day evocative of Chiara's elaborate Rococo taste and a fine example of the general mania for redecoration that swept Venice in the eighteenth century. Generations of relative neglect have preserved the authenticity of the details and general scheme – electricity was never introduced into the state apartments – but the gradual restoration taken in hand by the present owners is all the more complicated as a result. The house is still owned by descendants of the last Pisani of San Tomà.

80. The late fifteenth-century tracery and balconies of Palazzo Pisani-Moretta

Palazzo Contarini-Corfu and Palazzo Contarini degli Scrigni

Two of the virtually innumerable palaces of the Contarini family stand together on the right bank of the Grand Canal just above the Accademia bridge in the parish of Santi Gervasio e Protasio, popularly known in Venice as San Trovaso. The first, approaching from the Rialto, is a Gothic house of the fifteenth century, with the traditional quatrefoil tracery derived from the upper loggia of the ducal palace providing the centre-piece of the *piano nobile* decoration. Other carved details are well made, especially the corner cable moulding and quoins, and the whole façade has a subtle colourism, probably the result of the seventeenth-century remodelling, with grey marble sheathing, faded red Verona marble in the wall space framing the Gothic windows, and square plaques of yellow- and grey-veined Brescian marble. The house is known as the Palazzo Contarini-Corfu and it is supposed that the name comes from a family called di Corfu that lived at San Trovaso before the Contarini built their house here. Others maintain that the palace takes its name from a Contarini who was a general of the armies on the island of Corfu.

The second house, the Palazzo Contarini degli Scrigni, belongs to a different type altogether. It was built in 1609 by Palladio's disciple, Vincenzo Scamozzi, and is thus out of chronological order here. But it is not a separate palace and must be considered with its neighbour. Despite the marked difference in their architectural styles and the gap in years between their construction, Scamozzi's building was meant as an adjunct to the Contarini-Corfu and thus exemplifies the Venetian practice of enlarging a house by adding a complete palace next door. Simple lateral enlargements incorporated in the original building can be seen at the Palazzo Sagredo, in the newer section of the Soranzo house at San Polo, in the sixteenth-century Palazzo Martinengo, and on the grandest scale in the Pisani and Labia palaces. The Soranzo, Giustinian and Mocenigo houses are proper double palaces, both units being built at more or less the same time and definitely in the same style. Palazzo Barbaro is the principal example illustrated here of the type of enlargement carried out for the Contarini at San Trovaso.

In both cases a seventeenth-century building was joined to a fifteenth-century Gothic house; and in both cases, the addition was made principally to give the owners more reception rooms. At the Palazzo Barbaro, Gaspari made the architecture of his addition subservient to the older house and linked the two by continuing his balconies across the façade of the Gothic house. Scamozzi essayed a palace apparently complete in itself, but reflecting the

81. Palazzo Contarini degli Scrigni seen from Palazzo Falier

dimensions and volumes of the older building. The result is not a complete success. Although in its proportions Scamozzi's palace is a complement to the Contarini-Corfu, the expanses of unconventional wall space covered in *pietra d'Istria* and the heavy rustication of the ground floor outweigh, instead of balancing, the delicacy of the adjacent house. The windows of the *piano nobile*, set at regular intervals with no central *portego* grouping, seem heavy and un-Venetian until one takes the internal plan into consideration. There was not meant to be a central *portego*, but rather two large salons running the length of the façade. Scamozzi has respected the requirements of his patrons, but his solution still seems awkward and out of place in Venice.

This branch of the Contarini took their name from the *scrigni*, or chests, found in the Villa Contarini at Piazzola on the Brenta when that house came into the family in 1418 as part of the dowry of Maria dei Carrara, daughter of Giacomo, lord of Padua, who married the philosopher, jurist, and ambassador Nicolò Contarini. Such an alliance between a Venetian patrician and the daughter of a reigning feudal lord was not exceptional and in earlier centuries Venetian nobles had even married daughters of the emperors of Byzantium. Like all branches of the public-spirited Contarini family, the degli Scrigni produced many remarkable servants of the Republic, such as Zaccaria, who held no fewer than sixty-three embassies in his lifetime.

In the early nineteenth century, the Contarini-Corfu and Scrigni palaces were inhabited by the last surviving member of the Contarini family, which only a generation earlier had numbered over eighteen branches in a flourishing family tree. This rapid and astonishing extinction of a numerous patrician family almost immediately after the fall of the Republic was not a unique case. Many noble families died out in the first thirty years after 1797. Legend has made much of family suicide pacts forbidding offspring to marry, but the fact is that only a few of a numerous Venetian noble family ever did marry, and with the collapse of the Republic's finances many aristocrats faced impoverishment, leaving daughters dowryless and sons without much hope of making a brilliant match. In any case, Alvise II Contarini, called Girolamo, was a worthy descendant of his distinguished forebears. A knight of the Golden Fleece, he bequeathed 184 paintings from his collection to the Academy gallery, including Bellini's *Madonna of the Alboretti*, and his extensive library to the Biblioteca Marciana. The remarkable furniture carved by Andrea Brustolon for the Contarini joined the collections of Teodoro Correr and today can be seen in the Ca' Rezzonico. Since Girolamo's death the Contarini palaces at San Trovaso have changed hands many times. The present owners live in the Contarini-Corfu, while the degli Scrigni palace has been divided and rented as apartments and office space.

RENAISSANCE PALACES

Palazzo Dario

The Palazzo Dario on the Grand Canal between the Academy bridge and the great votive church of the Madonna della Salute is one of the most frequently admired houses in Venice. Its charm lies in its size and decoration rather than in its relatively simple architecture. In the mind of the discriminating visitor, it is often rightly linked with the jewel-box church of Santa Maria dei Miracoli; both are products of the exquisite decorative taste of the Lombardo family. Its particularly Venetian qualities are even more obvious when one realizes that it was built at the same time as the Palazzo Strozzi in Florence. The Palazzo Dario has often been attributed to Pietro Lombardo, the founder of the dynasty that left its distinctive mark on early Venetian Renaissance architecture and sculpture. Although the architecture of the façade and many of its details are clearly of the early Renaissance, the marble sheathing, the use of roundels and plaques of porphyry, verde antico, and the mention of lapis lazuli in the old documents, reflect the colourism pervading Venetian decoration since the Veneto-Byzantine period.

The rich façade, added in 1487 to what was originally a Gothic house, was commissioned by Giovanni Dario, a chancery secretary of the Republic, who had been dispatched to the Sublime Porte in 1479 to conclude a peace treaty between the Venetians and the Sultan. Dario was responsible for negotiating, drafting and obtaining the signatures for the treaty. He did his work so well that the Republic rewarded him with the gift of a property near Padua worth some 1,500 ducats. The Sultan was also pleased with Dario's work, even though the treaty cost him the town of Scutari, and he presented the Venetian secretary with three robes of cloth of gold. Normally, the negotiating of an important treaty at Constantinople was the work of the *bailo*, the resident Venetian ambassador, whose special privileges dated from the days of Byzantium. The *bailo*'s rank of *primus inter pares,* or foremost among ambassadors, was generally respected by the Turks, and the Venetians considered it their most important diplomatic post. But from 1463 until 1479, when Dario's treaty was signed, the Republic had no *bailo* at Istanbul. The negotiation of a treaty by a secretary was unusual, but by no means unacceptable to the Turk. For years secretaries had been sent to Istanbul to settle all sorts of minor diplomatic details between the two great powers of the eastern Mediterranean.

The secretaries of the Republic were not recruited from the patriciate, but from the *cittadini originarii,* or citizen class. The citizens came from families often as ancient as those of the aristocracy, and citizenship became an exclusive

82. Palazzo Dario's richly encrusted façade at night

135

privilege restricted to those registered in the *Libro d'argento*, or Silver Book. Among the privileges of the citizen class was the right to work in the government chancery, and this hereditary prerogative meant that, though they might be excluded from voting and decision-making in the councils of state, they were none the less privy to the most secret of their deliberations. The secretary of an embassy might serve under several ambassadors, assisting each incumbent with his expertise. Drafting documents, letters, treaties, laws and judgements required proficiency in the fashionable Ciceronian Latin, as well as in Italian, Venetian and other languages, and chancery officials had to be highly educated. They, more than the patricians, were schooled in the disciplines of Aristotelian thought, Petrarchan humanism, and the quadrivium of scholasticism. In their case, and thus for Venetian higher education in general, the New Learning was a matter of practical training and application in the service of the state. Humanistic thinking and speculation as an end in itself never became characteristic of the Venetian Renaissance. Her chancery officials were never honoured for their learned treatises, perhaps because individual talents could be rewarded with one of the highest dignities of the state, the Grand Chancellorship. The *Gran Cancelliere* enjoyed precedence in the ceremonials of the Republic above the entire patriciate, its senators and procurators, and in procession marched alone before the doge himself.

Giovanni's learning and dedication to the state is implicit in the Latin motto he chose to have carved across the ground-floor façade of his house at San Gregorio. The lettering is of the most classical Roman type and the inscription proclaims that 'Giovanni Dario [dedicates his house] to the spirit of the city'. The marble-encrusted façade of the palazzo was obviously a costly affair for a secretary of the chancery, but investment and commercial opportunities in Venice were by no means the exclusive property of the patriciate. Mercantile *colleganze*, or investment partnerships, might involve as many as one hundred partners trusting their money to a dozen merchants shipping cargo to the Levant. While it was true in the fourteenth century that four times as many nobles as citizens were outstandingly rich, the moderately rich were about equally divided between these two classes. Many nobles were not rich at all, whereas numerous citizens had substantial holdings through their commercial investments. Giovanni Dario was obviously well off, and his reward for services to the state, his property near Padua, produced the equivalent of a modern pension; in addition he was given 600 ducats as a dowry for his illegitimate daughter when she married the patrician Vincenzo Barbaro in 1493.

The Palazzo Dario remained the property of this branch of the Barbaro family until the early nineteenth century, when it was sold to an Armenian diamond merchant. From 1838 to 1842 it was owned by Ruskin's friend, Rawdon Brown, who virtually bankrupted himself trying to restore it. Finally, he was forced to sell it to an official of the imperial government, Count Zichy, who in turn sold it to another member of the Austrian administration, Count Buol. Like so many other palaces in Venice, it suffered periods of neglect in the nineteenth century and the nadir came when it was transformed into a *pensione*. It was rescued from its degradation by the Comtesse de la Baume-Pluvinel, who restored it and lived in it with an affection attested by her frequent houseguest, the poet and memorialist, Henri de Régnier. In this century it has changed hands several times and is, at present, privately owned.

83. Palazzo Dario seen from Palazzo Corner della Ca' Grande

Palazzo Contarini-Polignac

The Palazzo Polignac near the Academy bridge was known to the Venetians of the Republic as the Palazzo Contarini dal Zaffo near the Carità. The Carità was the complex of church, conventual buildings, and cloisters, as well as a Scuola Grande, that was secularized and transformed into the Accademia under Napoleon's viceroy, Eugène de Beauharnais. The Palazzo Contarini-Polignac, as it may be styled, is one of the finest early Renaissance palaces in Venice. It provides the link between the decorative, sculpturesque style of the Lombardo family as seen at the Palazzo Dario and the later Albertian classicism of the Bergamasque architect, Mauro Coducci. In fact, its façade has been attributed to that intermediary figure in Venetian architecture, Giovanni Buora from Como, who worked with the Lombardo family at the Scuola Grande di San Marco and later collaborated with Mauro Coducci.

As at the Palazzo Dario, the Renaissance façade was added on to a Gothic building about which little is known. The continuing use of precious marble roundels links this façade to the Lombardesque style, but at the Palazzo Polignac, the plaques are used as symmetrical accents in the architecture and not primarily for colourism or richness of display. Symmetry through the use of both architectural and decorative elements is the key to the entire façade. Even the tall round-arched windows of the first and second principal floors are repeated for the sake of symmetry on the ground floor, where one might expect less important openings. The *piano nobile* frieze and the acroteria-type finials of the windows are carved with a sensitivity which again recalls the style of the Lombardo, but the fluted pilasters and the attempt at a classically correct cornice anticipate later developments.

Relatively little is known of the early ownership of this late fifteenth-century house, nor is it certain for whom it was built. It was bought by a member of the Contarini dal Zaffo family sometime between 1562 and 1582. In 1562 a certain Giorgio Contarini asked the Republic's permission to sell one-third of his feudal holdings in Cyprus, which since the extinction of the Lusignan dynasty he had held in fief to the Republic. In his request, he stated his intention to re-invest the proceeds from the sale in another entailed property, very probably the palace at the Carità. Giorgio belonged to the branch of the Contarini family known as dal Zaffo, the Venetian dialect rendering of Jaffa in the Levant, where the Contarini had extensive feudal holdings. Although not permitted to style themselves dukes of Jaffa in Venice, they could, like the Corner Piscopia or the Querini Stampalia, join the name of their fief to their surname. Each branch of the Contarini family quartered

84. The carved and decorated façade of Palazzo Contarini-Polignac seen from Palazzo Cavalli

Palazzo Contarini-Polignac

or charged its arms with various differences. The double-headed eagle of the empire or the lilies of France were differences bestowed on various Contarini after successful embassies. The Contarini were also hereditary knights of San Marco, the only chivalresque order bestowed by the Republic. It was generally an individual distinction, signified by a golden stole or toga worn on the left shoulder over the robes of office and by the initials KR added after the surname. Only in the Morosini, Querini, and Contarini families was the knighthood of San Marco hereditary – until the Rezzonico family was included in the eighteenth century.

The Contarini were one of the most ancient of the Republic's families. They and eleven other Venetian clans were called the 'apostolic families', a reference to their presence at the election of the first doge in 697. The Contarini traced their name and race to the Roman *gens* Aurelia Cotta, the family of Caesar's mother. Members of this dynasty became prefects of the Rhine and their family name and territorial jurisdiction were contracted into Cotta Rheni or possibly conti del Reno (Counts of the Rhine). In the service of the Venetian Republic, they provided eight doges, more than any other family: one each in the eleventh, thirteenth, and fourteenth centuries, and a virtual dynastic succession of five in the seventeenth century. Their combined reigns covered almost a century of the Republic's 1,100-year history.

One of the most interesting members of the Contarini dal Zaffo branch, Cardinal Gasparo Contarini, was an early advocate of curial reform in the Catholic Church. For his native city he produced a book called *Commonwealth and Government of Venice*, which attracted a wide readership and was translated into English as early as 1598. His San Giorgio circle, whose deliberations influenced the Council of Trent, included among its luminaries the learned Reginald Pole, later Mary Tudor's archbishop of Canterbury, as well as the forceful cleric, Giampietro Caraffa, who later became Pope Paul IV. Though of the same branch of the Contarini as those who lived at the Carità, Gasparo's family house was located near the Madonna dell'Orto, where he was buried in 1542.

Late in the eighteenth century, the Palazzo Contarini dal Zaffo was sold to Domenico Manzoni, whose success in the revived Venetian silk trade had made him a rich man and the proprietor of two feudal holdings in the Friuli. The Manzoni family lived here until the early nineteenth century, when the house was sold to a widow of the Angaran family of Vicenza. Later the palace changed hands many times and was eventually bought by the Prince and Princesse Edmond de Polignac in the early years of this century. Princesse de Polignac was a painter, musician and imaginative patron of the arts. Her life-long interest in painting encompassed the friendship of Sargent and Picasso and she established in her palace on the Grand Canal a salon worthy of the famous eighteenth-century hostesses of the Republic. Her memory is preserved in Venice in the name of her house, the Palazzo de Polignac, which is still owned by her family.

85. Palazzo Polignac seen from the garden of Palazzo Cavalli

Palazzo Corner-Spinelli

The Palazzo Corner-Spinelli on the Grand Canal in the parish of Sant'Angelo was built between 1490 and 1510 by the Bergamasque stonecutter-architect, Mauro Coducci. It is one of the first examples of a distinct Renaissance architectural personality in Venice. Coducci had worked with the Lombardo family of architects at the Scuola Grande di San Marco, where he and Giovanni Buora, the architect of the Palazzo Contarini-Polignac, collaborated on the completion of the work designed by Pietro Lombardo and his sons. The Lombardesque influence is still discernible at the Corner-Spinelli, especially in the traditional Venetian use of polychrome marble plaques, but like Buora at the Palazzo Contarini-Polignac, Coducci treats these pieces of colouristic decoration as subsidiary to the rhythms of the architecture. The most striking influence on Coducci's personal architectural vocabulary came not from the local traditions and schools, but from the Florentine Leon Battista Alberti, with whom he may have worked on the Tempio Malatestiano in Rimini. The marked horizontalism of the Corner-Spinelli façade might be interpreted as an Albertian element, but the horizontal zones of the Venetian Gothic palace must also be kept in mind; certainly the rustication of the ground floor is in the Tuscan taste, even though executed with Venetian conservatism. The Codussian window (two round-arched lights framed in a larger single round arch, the resultant spandrel filled with a circular or, in this case, drop-shaped piercing) can be traced directly to the windows of Alberti's Palazzo Rucellai in Florence and from there back to earlier Tuscan and Romanesque prototypes. But Coducci's windows are not only bolder than Alberti's, they also have something of the Venetian Gothic in them. The round arches and central piercing are not only fully moulded, but the whole composition and its execution is treated more like tracery than as a structural element. Coducci may have even had in mind the intersecting semicircle tracery of the Pisani-Moretta palace, which stands across the canal from the Corner-Spinelli. Certainly for another noteworthy detail of the house he did borrow from a specific late Gothic prototype: the trefoil-plan, projecting balconies of the lateral *piano nobile* windows are virtually copies of those on the fifteenth-century Casa Pigafetta in Vicenza. Coducci repeated his windows in other Venetian buildings, but the trefoil balconies make their only appearance in Venice at the Corner-Spinelli house. For all his influence on Venetian architecture, the Codussian window seems to have been considered too individualistic and perhaps too bold for conservative Venetian tastes; no other architect adopted it in later houses.

86. Mauro Coducci's Palazzo Corner-Spinelli, built between 1490 and 1510

THE CORNER OR CORNARO FAMILY

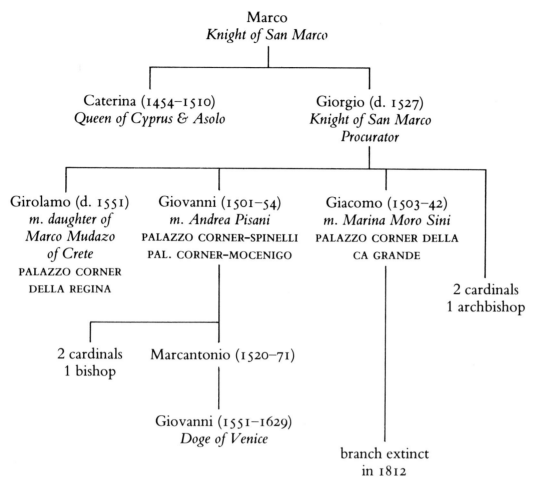

Marco
Knight of San Marco

Caterina (1454–1510)
Queen of Cyprus & Asolo

Giorgio (d. 1527)
Knight of San Marco
Procurator

Girolamo (d. 1551)
m. daughter of
Marco Mudazo
of Crete
PALAZZO CORNER
DELLA REGINA

Giovanni (1501–54)
m. Andrea Pisani
PALAZZO CORNER-SPINELLI
PAL. CORNER-MOCENIGO

Giacomo (1503–42)
m. Marina Moro Sini
PALAZZO CORNER DELLA
CA GRANDE

2 cardinals
1 archbishop

2 cardinals
1 bishop

Marcantonio (1520–71)

Giovanni (1551–1629)
Doge of Venice

branch extinct
in 1812

This simplified table is based on the charts of Oliver Logan, *Culture & Society in Venice 1470–1790*, London 1972 and Deborah Howard, *Jacopo Sansovino*, New Haven & London 1975

In the late 1530s the palace at Sant'Angelo was sold to senator Giovanni Corner, son of one of the Republic's richest men and nephew of Caterina Corner, Queen of Cyprus. Giovanni had originally settled in a house at San Polo, but a fire destroyed it in 1535. He commissioned Michele Sanmicheli to build another palace for him on the site, and in the meantime, he bought Coducci's palace from the Lando family. At Sant'Angelo, he embarked on redecoration and employed Sanmicheli to remodel Coducci's *andron*. The Veronese architect transformed the traditionally plain Venetian water-gate hall into a Roman atrium with Tuscan Doric columns and pilasters, a Serlian round-arch motif opening onto the garden, a courtyard, and a side water-gate. Sanmicheli's use of the Serlian motif as a wall decoration at the Palazzo Corner-Spinelli is a restrained and rather two-dimensional anticipation of his barrel-vaulted Serlian atrium at the Grimani palace in nearby San Luca. Through Sanmicheli, Giovanni Corner also obtained the services of Giorgio Vasari, who was visiting Venice and who painted nine panels for an elaborate ceiling; this has since been broken up and dispersed, but some of the panels have been identified in various collections. Contemporary documents mention other rich ceiling decoration and one room still contains a richly coffered and gilt carved ceiling which may have been part of the original decoration.

Giovanni Corner's descendants at Sant'Angelo were succeeded in the ownership of the house by the Spinelli family who, like the Manzoni of the Palazzo Contarini-Polignac, became rich through the Republic's seventeenth-century textile industry. The Spinelli were Venetians of the citizen class and dealt in cloth of gold, silks, wools, and cloths dyed in rare purples and scarlets. In 1718, they offered 100,000 ducats to the Republic for their admission to the patriciate. By the mid-nineteenth century, the house was owned by Major Edward Cheney, an English friend of John and Effie Ruskin, who formed an important collection of the then unfashionable work of Gianbattista Tiepolo. The house has changed owners many times in recent years. It is now divided into apartments and is well maintained. In keeping with the Spinelli's trade, the *piano nobile* serves as the headquarters of one of Venice's most important textile manufacturers.

87. The Codussian windows and distinctive ground floor rustication of Palazzo Corner-Spinelli

146

Palazzo Vendramin-Calergi

The Palazzo Loredan at San Marcuola, now known to the Venetians as the Palazzo Vendramin-Calergi and to visitors as the Municipal Casino, is one of the most magnificent palaces in the city. Approached either from the upper Grand Canal or from the Rialto, it rises a full seventy-eight Venetian feet (22 metres) above the canal. It is the masterpiece of Mauro Coducci, who began it for the Loredan some time after 1500; it was completed after his death in 1504 by stonecutters of the Lombardo workshop. Like Coducci's Palazzo Corner-Spinelli, the façade is entirely covered with Istrian stone, though here there is no rustication on the ground floor, but instead a handsome pilaster motif like the one that Sanmicheli used later at the Grimani palace at San Luca. The horizontalism of the house is striking, emphasized as it is by continuous balconies, a tall, unbroken frieze, and a projecting cornice worthy of any great Florentine palace. The Codussian windows are a prominent part of the design, but, with doubled columns to disguise the irregular intervals of the conventional Venetian palace façade, their vertical elements contribute to the impression of a continuous arcade. Despite its massive harmonies, the delicacy of the Lombardesque influence on Coducci's work is still evident in the finely carved capitals, the heraldic eagles and shields of the frieze, and in the handsome classical lettering of the Loredan motto, NON NOBIS DOMINE, carved across the ground-floor walls.

The patrician Loredan family had, like most Venetian noble families, several palaces in the city at any given time, but a résumé of the history of this powerful clan belongs more properly to their house in Santo Stefano, the home of the first of their three doges. In any case, the Loredan lived at San Marcuola for less than eighty years; but in that short space of time they left their mark on the house and on the history of artistic patronage in Venice's golden age. They had the ground-floor entrance of the palace frescoed with allegorical figures, coats of arms, and friezes by Giorgione, and work was commissioned from Titian as well. In 1581 they sold the house to Heinrich, duke of Brunswick, for 60,000 ducats. Two years later it was sold to the family of Guglielmo Gonzaga, Duke of Mantua, for 90,000, but a quarrel with the Brunswick heirs resulted in a complicated litigation and the palace was finally sold at auction to Vittore Calergi, who paid only 36,000 ducats for it. The Calergi were an extremely rich family originally from Candia in Crete. Their submission to the Venetians in 1258 had not only preserved their immense patrimony, but had also made them eligible for inclusion in the patriciate. After contributing vast sums to the Republic's wars against Genoa, they were inscribed in the Golden Book in 1381.

88. Palazzo Vendramin-Calergi, built for the Loredan by Mauro Coducci in the first decade of the sixteenth century

89. Detail of an engraving showing the cornice

Palazzo Vendramin-Calergi

The riches of the Calergi were such that successive owners of Coducci's Palazzo Loredan agreed to join the name Calergi to their own family names. In 1594 Vittore's daughter and sole heiress, Marina, married Vincenzo Grimani, thus founding the family known as the Grimani-Calergi, which lived at San Marcuola for over one hundred years. In the early seventeenth century Marina commissioned Vincenzo Scamozzi to enlarge the palace with a wing to the right of the façade. Her sons, Giovanni and Pietro, braving a sentence of banishment from Venice for various misdemeanours, hid out in the new wing of the house. Harbouring an implacable hatred for Francesco Querini-Stampalia, they had him kidnapped from his gondola one night and dragged to the palace. There he was murdered by their hired *bravi*, a combination of bodyguard and footpad employed by many Venetian nobles. Since they did not commit the murder themselves, the Republic could only lengthen the term of their banishment and see that it was enforced, but such was the outcry against the crime that the Scamozzi wing of the house was razed to the ground and a column of infamy erected on the site.

In 1738 the last of the Grimani-Calergi left the house to Nicolò Vendramin, again with the stipulation that the name Calergi should be perpetuated. Like the Calergi, the Vendramin had been ennobled after the war of Chioggia in

91. The lower loggia of Fondaco dei Turchi, with Palazzo Vendramin-Calergi (left)

90. Palazzo Vendramin-Calergi

Palazzo Vendramin-Calergi

1381. They were bankers at the Rialto and well known for their riches. In 1476 a member of the family, Andrea, was elected doge and on his death a splendid tomb designed and carved by Tullio Lombardo was set up in the church of the Servite friars. When the church was destroyed in the early nineteenth century, fragments of the tomb, including the famous *Adam* now in the Metropolitan Museum, were brought to the Vendramin-Calergi palace. These pieces of sculpture were displayed on the *piano nobile* in a hall which was decorated with jasper columns taken from a temple at Ephesus. The rest of the tomb and the doge's remains were placed in the church of Santi Giovanni e Paolo.

In 1845, Nicolò Vendramin-Calergi sold the palace to Maria Carolina, widow of the Duc de Berry, pretender to the throne of his father, King Charles X of France. By the time she decided to settle at San Marcuola, Maria Carolina had already married her paramour, the Sicilian Count Enrico Lucchesi-Palli. She brought up her Bourbon son, the Comte de Chambord, with the numerous children of her morganatic husband, who was now styled the Duca della Grazia. H.R.H. the Duchesse de Berry, as she liked to be known and as history and the Venetians have remembered her, held splendid court at San Marcuola. She also installed a fine collection of old masters. But after ten years in the house, Chambord realized that his mother's extravagance might easily prove ruinous and conspired to have the palace declared a bailiwick of the Sovereign Military Order of Malta, thus effectively blocking its enlargement, redecoration, or sale. But Maria Carolina was not to be baulked of her splendid and extravagant life. After another ten years, Chambord at last forced her to sell much of the contents of the house at two days of sales held in the Hôtel Drouot in Paris. She died five years later, and the ownership of the house devolved on her Lucchesi-Palli heirs.

Although the della Grazia dukes lived in a grand style, too, they did not use all of the immense house, and in September 1882 they arranged to let fifteen of the mezzanine rooms of the garden wing to Richard Wagner. In November, Wagner was joined by his father-in-law, Franz Liszt, who there composed *La lugubre gondola*, and on Christmas Eve the two men gave a private concert at the Fenice opera house. On 13 February 1883 Wagner suffered a stroke and died in his wife's arms. Franz Werfel has given substance to the legend that Verdi, who was in Venice, came to the Palazzo Vendramin on that very afternoon to pay his respects to the master he so admired and whom he had never met. In memory of the great composer who had died in their house, the della Grazia dukes organized annual concerts of Wagner's music, performed in the garden by the municipal band.

In 1926, having managed to transfer the bailiwick of the Knights of Malta to a villa in the country, Count Volpi di Misurata bought the palazzo. After the Second World War it was bought by the municipality of Venice and one of the three gambling casinos licensed in Italy was established in it. However, in unintentional imitation of the Republic's old gambling laws, Venetian residents are forbidden to enter and gamble at the Palazzo Vendramin-Calergi.

Palazzo Contarini delle Figure

In some instances an architectural feature of a palace was taken to distinguish a particular branch of a patrician family: thus Barbarigo della Terrazza, Michiel delle Colonne, Contarini dalla Porta di Ferro and Contarini delle Figure. There has been speculation as to which 'figures' distinguish the Contarini palace at San Samuel, but it is generally agreed that the two tiny caryatids under the *portego* balcony are the most likely candidates. This house at the *volta del canal*, whose architecture is neither as delicate as the Lombardesque nor as bold as the creations of Sansovino, represents a bridge or transition between these two distinctive schools and styles.

The Palazzo Contarini delle Figure was begun in about 1504, probably by the Venetian architect, Giorgio Spavento, and brought to completion before 1546 by Antonio Abbondi, called Lo Scarpignino, the dialect word for 'stonecutter'. These two men, little known outside Venice, carried out important commissions in the city that illustrate their position between the Lombardesque and the High Renaissance periods of Venetian architecture. Spavento began work on San Salvador with members of the Lombardo workshop, and the church was brought to completion by Sansovino. Abbondi completed the work begun by Bartolomeo Bon at the Scuola di San Rocco; his own commission for San Fantin and for the new building at the Rialto were both completed by Sansovino. Spavento and Lo Scarpignino collaborated on the construction of the emporium of the German merchants (the Fondaco dei Tedeschi) at the Rialto, but more relevant to the Palazzo Contarini delle Figure was their work together at the Ducal Palace. They both worked on the reconstruction of the east wing of the palace after a fire in 1483 had destroyed that part of the old building. The aedicular windows of the graceful little Senators' chapel are the prototypes of the lateral windows of the *piano nobile* of the Contarini house at San Samuel. But the marble sheathing of the palace façade, and particularly the use of yellow- and grey-veined marble at the second *piano nobile*, and the round-arched windows there, recall Lombardesque work such as that of Giovanni Buora at the Palazzo Contarini-Polignac. While the beribboned marble plaques and the heraldic trophies, remarked on by Ruskin, are decorative motifs like those popular with the Lombardo, the use of pilasters and especially the bold pediment supported by antique fluted columns for the *piano nobile portego* suggest an architectural classicism that foreshadows later developments.

The member of the Contarini family most often associated with the house at San Samuel was Jacopo (or Giacomo, 1536–95), the son of Pietro, who had

151

Palazzo Contarini delle Figure

the palace built. It was Jacopo who made the house a repository of patrician learning and patronage. On the *piano nobile* he assembled a collection including paintings by the Bassani, Titian, Tintoretto, the followers of Giorgione, and Palma il Giovane. He was also a patron of Renaissance studies in mathematics and had an extensive collection of mathematical and cosmographical instruments as well as a remarkable library. He also seems to have been something of a botanist and his garden at San Samuel was famous for its variety of subtropical plants brought from the Levant. Jacopo's knowledge of architecture resulted in his close friendship with Palladio, who often stayed in the house. In 1574, the year he was made a senator, Jacopo was asked to help organize the festivities in honour of the state visit of Henry III of France. Besides giving commissions to Veronese, Vittoria, Sansovino, and the aged Titian, he commissioned from his friend Palladio the famous triumphal arch at the Lido under which the French monarch received the doge's homage and welcome. In 1577 Jacopo's learning and taste were again called to the service of the Republic: he was asked to draw up a programme of historical paintings for the hall of the Great Council, the hall of the Scrutiny, and the senators' antechamber to replace those lost in the fire of that year.

In 1580 Jacopo inherited a large number of drawings from the estate of his friend Palladio and fifteen years later, in his own will, he bequeathed all his collections to his heirs, but with the proviso that should his branch fail in the male line, all the treasures of the Palazzo Contarini should pass to the Great Council of the Republic. Jacopo had a worthy heir to carry out his instructions. In 1712, Bertucci, the last of the Contarini delle Figure, died and his will was read, in accordance with Venetian patrician custom, in the presence of the corpse. He had repeated both in letter and spirit his ancestor's dispositions, for he bequeathed to the state much that had been acquired in his branch since 1595 as well. As befitted the self-effacement of this last Contarini, he left instructions that there was to be no public announcement of his death, and that he be buried entirely without pomp, dressed in the habit of a Capuchin friar, at the Redentore church, which had been built on land given to the state by another of his ancestors. The Marcian library benefited enormously from the Contarini bequest, but perhaps the best-known example of their legacy is Veronese's *Rape of Europa*, which now hangs in the antechamber of the doge's council room. Palladio's drawings somehow made their way to England, probably through the agents of Lord Burlington, and now form part of the collections of the Royal Institute of British Architects.

In the nineteenth century the house was owned by the marchesi Guiccioli of Ravenna. They were kinsmen of Alessandro Guiccioli, whose wife Teresa had been the famous last attachment of Lord Byron, an affair that began in 1819, when the poet had apartments in the neighbouring Mocenigo houses at San Samuel. In 1880 Richard Wagner spent the month of October here, installed in what his wife Cosima regarded as unnecessary extravagance and surrounded by numerous retainers, hangers-on, and family. The Palazzo Contarini is still a private house, though divided into flats.

92. The early sixteenth-century Palazzo Contarini delle Figure

Palazzo Loredan at Santo Stefano

The long, low Palazzo Loredan in the campo Santo Stefano was originally a house of Gothic design belonging to the Mocenigo family. Little remains of that palace save a few traces of stone on the rio façade and a well-head. From old maps we know that it was large, but nothing like as long as the present house. The Loredan bought it in 1536 and soon after hired Antonio Abbondi to remodel it. To him are due the eight round-arched windows of the *portego* and five windows on either side, but as can be seen from the surviving tiny Gothic rain-spouts under the *portego* windows, he was probably doing no more than modernizing the outlines of the former building. By Venetian standards the palace was extremely long, and it seemed even longer when in the early seventeenth century four more windows were added to the northern end of the façade to light the recently built ballroom. On the north end Giovanni Grapiglia added a Palladian façade in Istrian stone. For years this fine classical façade was attributed to Palladio himself, but it has recently been correctly identified as the work of the architect whom the Loredan commissioned to design the tomb of their most illustrious doge, Leonardo, in the church of Santi Giovanni e Paolo.

93. Palazzo Contarini delle Figure seen from Palazzo Civran-Grimani

94. The Neptune door-knocker, designed by Alessandro Vittoria, at Palazzo Loredan

The Loredan were supposedly known in Roman times as the Mainardi, a contraction of *manum ardeo*, alluding to their legendary ancestor, Gaius Mucius Scaevola, who demonstrated his courage and indifference to physical pain by calmly plunging his hand into fire. A representation of this scene, along with other episodes of mythical Roman history, once existed in frescoes by Salviati on the long façade of the palace. The Mainardi eventually became known to the Romans as the Laureati from their many laurel-crowned triumphs and victories. The Loredan were established in Venice by 1015 and were among the first patrician families registered in the Golden Book of 1297.

Most famous of the many illustrious Loredan was perhaps Pietro, three times capitan-general da mar, whose fleets ranged over much of Dalmatia in the early fifteenth century and who engineered a victory over combined Milanese and Genoese naval forces. In 1416 he commanded the Venetian fleet in the great battle against the Turk at Gallipolli. He was several times wounded by arrows, but fought bravely on until the Turkish forces had been routed and their admiral killed. Many of the enemy committed suicide in shame over the tremendous defeat, but Loredan captured numerous European recruits from among them, including a rebel Venetian, Giorgio Calergi, whom he had quartered on the poop of his own ship.

Despite Pietro's fame among the Venetians, the most widely recognized of

95. Palazzo Loredan at Santo Stefano – a section of the long façade seen from the Campo

the Loredan, were he to walk the streets of Venice again, would surely be Doge Leonardo Loredan, whose splendid azure and gold portrait by Giovanni Bellini now hangs in the National Gallery in London. Leonardo deserves to be known for more than his likeness. He was doge of Venice in its darkest days (1501–21) and can be said to have preserved the state from total collapse. It was during his reign that Venice reaped the first bitter rewards of the expansionist policies of the Doges Tommaso Mocenigo and Francesco Foscari. The fifteenth-century mainland expansion of the Republic had been watched with annoyance and envy by other European states until halting the Venetian encroachments became the common cause of them all. United by virulent propaganda against the Republic (propaganda which still gets a hearing from supposedly serious historians of Venice), the pope, the emperor, and the kings of France and Spain joined in a league against the Venetians. The League of Cambrai, as their alliance was known, inflicted defeat after defeat, the *Dominante* watching helpless as her subject towns offered a loyal but ineffective resistance to superior forces. When the conquest of the Republic seemed almost complete, in 1509, Venice began to deploy her most subtle weapon, diplomacy: she played on the personalities and ambitions of Pope Julius II and the emperor Maximilian and their allies until they were divided

96. The sixteenth-century façade screen of Palazzo Loredan at Santo Stefano

156

among themselves. In subsequent treaties Venice recovered some of the surrendered territories and in an even more remarkable defeat of the League's propaganda, many of the mainland cities offered themselves to the *Dominante* of their own free will. The Venetians long saw in the gaunt and resolute features of their doge suffering and the determination of their Republic to survive the hostility of the mightiest powers in Europe, and Leonardo Loredan's portrait figures in any number of the allegorical paintings commissioned by the grateful Republic.

The legend that Leonardo was born in the palace at Santo Stefano has been disproved, but his branch of the family did live there and there is no good reason to doubt Ridolfi's assertion in the seventeenth century that the doge sat to Bellini for his portrait in a room in this house. In the early sixteenth century, the campo Santo Stefano, one of the largest in Venice, became famous for the festivities organized there. Tournaments with jousting are mentioned in the chronicles and a pavement in the centre of the square called the Liston gave its name to the Venetian evening promenade. As recently as 1802 the last *caccia ai tori*, a popular kind of bull-baiting, took place at Santo Stefano. The collapse of a grandstand of spectators led to a ban on the sport in the city. After the fall of the Republic, the Loredan palace at Santo Stefano served various official functions. It was the seat of the Austrian military governor for a time and in 1865 it housed the Imperial and Royal Provincial Delegation. After the Unification of Italy it became the headquarters of the Royal Carabinieri and in 1892 it was purchased to house the Veneto Institute of Science, Letters and Arts, which had been founded under the Napoleonic administration. This learned society, well known in Italy for its scholarly publications, still has its seat in the Palazzo Loredan.

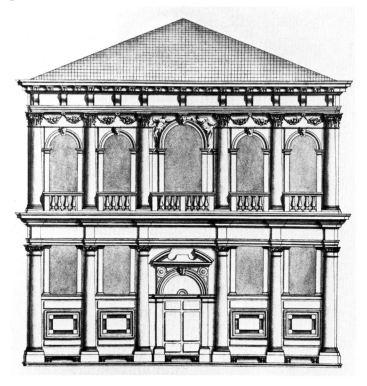

97. An engraving of Palazzo Loredan at Santo Stefano (Visentini: *Venetian Palaces,* I, British Museum)

Palazzo Martinengo

The plain, simple façade of the Palazzo Martinengo on the Grand Canal might easily be overlooked by the visitor to Venice. Architecturally the palace is of interest because it is one of the few that preserve the proportions of some of the oldest houses. Though built in the early sixteenth century, it has only one *piano nobile* and thus is in scale with the approximate dimensions of the much earlier Veneto-Byzantine houses that were only two storeys high. Besides this curious anachronism and coincidence, the palace is one of those that were enlarged with a lateral addition. The left wing, built in about 1663, is only one room long, but this room is of generous dimensions and its *portego-* like window group is given such prominence in the façade that the wing was obviously intended to provide an important reception room in the manner of Scamozzi's earlier addition to the Palazzo Contarini-Corfu. But a visitor in the days of the Republic could hardly have failed to notice and admire the Palazzo Martinengo. Soon after it was built for the Talenti family, it passed to Martino d'Anna, a rich Flemish merchant, patron of the arts, and, according to legend, Titian's godson. It was probably he who ordered the overall fresco decoration by Pordenone (died 1539), which must have been, together with Tintoretto's fresco for the Gussoni at Santa Sofia and Salviati's for the Loredan at Santo Stefano, one of the most remarkable palace façade decorations in the city.

The Palazzo Martinengo is interesting for another feature of its architecture and as an illustration of the way in which some Venetian houses become an inextricable part of an adjacent building. Like the Palazzo Labia at San Geremia, the back of the Palazzo Martinengo is built virtually around its parish church. This was due to the extension of the *calle* side of the house, which reaches back to the campo di San Beneto with the small Benedictine church that the house almost encloses. There are still two windows in the palace that open into and are part of the clerestory of the small church. The interior plan of the Martinengo palace is conventionally Venetian save for the enfilade of rooms added on to the canal front and along the *calle*. The handsomely decorated and well maintained rooms give an excellent idea of the traditional furnishing of a palace of the Republic. Even the fine Empire furniture of the library and the delightful nineteenth-century atmosphere of the ballroom seem in keeping with Venetian patrician taste.

The house changed hands many times in the days of the Republic. From the family of Martino d'Anna it passed to the Viaro, Foscarini, and Martinengo families. It seems only fitting that the palace should be remembered by the

98. OVERLEAF LEFT The once-frescoed, mid-sixteenth-century façade of Palazzo Martinengo

99. OVERLEAF RIGHT The library of Palazzo Martinengo, showing the early terrazzo floor and furniture of the First Empire

159

Palazzo Martinengo

name of the last. The Martinengo were great feudal landowners in the Venetian territories of Brescia. The founder of the family was one Teobaldo, who as favourite of the emperor Otto I was made imperial vicar and given fifteen castles near Brescia. His grandson built the famous castle of Martinengo and his descendants made their name as fighting men. Four times they were admitted to the Venetian patriciate, three times as *condottieri* for the armies of the Republic and once, in 1689, for the statutory contribution of 100,000 ducats towards the war against the Turk at Candia. As Venetian patricians they settled first at San Marcuola and then at San Beneto. The house remained in their hands until the nineteenth century, when it was bought by Giovanni Conti, who on his death in 1872 bequeathed it to a hospital. The administrators of the hospital sold it again in 1883. Early in this century it was bought by Count Volpi di Misurata.

The name of Count Volpi has become one of the most controversial in the recent history of Venice. It was he who planned and founded the industrial port of Mestre–Marghera at about the same time he bought this house for his family. His original idea was a splendid one: to revive Venice economically along the lines of maritime commerce that had once enriched the Republic. His initiative was public-spirited, and he could have hardly foreseen at that early date that, instead of bringing employment to Venetians who would commute from Venice to their mainland jobs, Mestre would end by depopulating the historic centre and threatening with its noxious effluents the very city he loved. The essentially economic link between Mestre and Venice was codified in the period before the Second World War by combining their municipal administrations. Today this arrangement has lost its original sense, since two-thirds of the municipal population live in Mestre and its environs, and the taxes paid by the Venetians in the ancient centre will inevitably be spent where most of the voters live. The industries of Mestre–Marghera support too many Venetians ever to be abolished or even much reduced, but were the municipality once again to be divided in two, the separate and sometimes conflicting needs of the two towns might be more effectively met.

Palazzo Gussoni-Grimani

The Palazzo Gussoni-Grimani on the Grand Canal in the parish of San Felice was attributed to Michele Sanmicheli of Verona as early as the seventeenth century, and the attribution has recently been reaffirmed. The reader of old guide books and documents is often bemused by the number of unimportant buildings attributed to architects such as Sanmicheli, Scamozzi, and even Palladio. But the Gussoni house is not unimportant, only less obviously striking than some of the others. The architect who built it between 1548 and 1556 was probably instructed by his patron to keep it simple and to leave as much wall space on the façade as possible. The Palazzo Gussoni, along with the Palazzo Martinengo, was meant to have a frescoed façade. To fresco a water-front façade in Venice must have been considered every bit as sumptuous as to cover an elaborate classical façade in Istrian stone. Often the greatest artists of the day were employed, such as Titian and Giorgione, who worked in fresco at the Fondaco dei Tedeschi. Though traces remained of the Gussoni frescoes as late as the eighteenth century, Jacopo Tintoretto's two figures inspired by Michelangelo's *Dawn* and *Dusk* from the Medici tombs have now completely disappeared. Fresco work imitating famous sculpture seems to have been popular in Venice and old documents speak of Tintoretto painting a version of the Colleoni equestrian monument as a *trompe l'oeil* on a chimney in Santo Stefano. Giovanni Battista Zelotti, who frescoed many halls in Palladio's villas, did a series imitating antique statues of gladiators for the courtyard of the Palazzo Gussoni. But even with all trace of the frescoes gone, the palace is a handsome building. Its proportions are extremely well balanced and it marks one of the first appearances of rectangular instead of arched lateral windows in a Venetian palace façade. Segmental or triangular pediments above such windows became a popular motif for a whole series of late sixteenth- and seventeenth-century palaces.

The Gussoni, who had the house built, or perhaps ordered the rebuilding of an older house, were among the ancient families of the Republic. Coming to the lagoon from the mainland with the other refugees from the barbarian invasions, they first settled at Torcello. From there they came to Venice, where they founded the church of Santa Sofia in 1050; long their parish church, the building was dedicated in the Byzantine manner to the Holy Wisdom and not to a saint named Sophia. One of the Gussoni was with Doge Enrico Dandolo at the conquest of Zara and the subsequent siege and capture of Constantinople itself during the so-called Fourth Crusade. The house at San Felice remained in their hands until the eighteenth century.

100. OVERLEAF LEFT The *portego* of Palazzo Martinengo

101. OVERLEAF RIGHT The *andron* of Palazzo Martinengo looking towards the main staircase and the courtyard

For English visitors, its most interesting associations are with the second embassy of Sir Henry Wotton, who lived in the Palazzo Gussoni from 1614 to 1618. Sir Henry was a fervent Anglican and during his first embassy from James I in 1605, he became embroiled in the excommunication of Venice by Pope Paul V. He was frustrated in his attempts to bring Venice over to the Protestant side even though his scheme seemed to enjoy the encouragement of the Republic's remarkable theological adviser, Fra Paolo Sarpi. In 1618, during his second embassy, the Spanish viceroy of Naples, the Duke of Osuna, with the collaboration of his colleague at Milan, attempted to capture and overthrow the government of Venice herself with a combination of internal conspiracy and treachery, backed by the viceregal fleet in the Adriatic. The plot was discovered in time and the viceroy's ships scattered on the first appearance of the British navy in the Mediterranean.

Wotton has left us valuable descriptions of his life in the Palazzo Gussoni, of his musical evenings, his Anglican chapel, the antics of his pet Barbary ape, his reading and study in the mezzanine library, and also of the decoration of the house. He mentions the armoury in the *andron*, the gilded leather wall hangings and brass tubs of aromatic spices in the *portego*, and the collection of paintings and massive furniture in the other rooms. As a foreign ambassador to the Most Serene Republic, he was treated with the utmost respect according to the protocols of a government which had virtually invented modern diplomacy and the idea of resident ambassadors. However, the same government forbade its patriciate all social contact with a foreign ambassador. This apparently xenophobic legislation is easier to understand when one considers that all patricians were members of the government and concourse with foreigners might lead to compromise or even betrayal of the Republic's policies and secrets. The learned Sir Henry's life in the Palazzo Gussoni was self-contained and slightly monastic, not unlike that of an Oxford college of his day. Young apprentice diplomats lived under his roof as did Englishmen who were travelling in Italy with letters from members of the English aristocracy and government – at that date, as in Venice, virtually one and the same. Life as an ambassador in seventeenth-century Venice as described in his dispatches and letters reminds one of life in today's diplomatic compounds of Moscow or Peking. It was Sir Henry who coined the phrase: 'An ambassador is an honest man sent to lie abroad for the good of his country.'

Wotton returned to England after a third embassy when the highlight of his residence was the execution of a Venetian patrician falsely accused of conspiratorial conversations with an English lady resident in the city. In his retirement as Provost of Eton, Wotton enjoyed the friendship of Izaak Walton, who wrote his biography, and he sent letters of advice to the young John Milton, who was then visiting Italy.

In the nineteenth century the English historian of Venice, Rawdon Brown, came to live at the Palazzo Gussoni because of its associations with Wotton and until recently the palace was owned by a family whose roots were in Sir Henry's native Kent.

102. Palazzo Gussoni seen from Palazzo Pesaro. The mid-sixteenth-century palace is attributed to Michele Sanmicheli and was once frescoed by Jacopo Tintoretto

103. OVERLEAF Canaletto: *Regatta on the Grand Canal*

167

Palazzo Grimani

The Palazzo Grimani in the parish of San Luca stands on the corner of the rio di San Luca and the Grand Canal below the Rialto bridge in the *sestiere* of San Marco. It is one of the great architectural monuments of Venice and arguably the masterpiece of the Veronese architect Michele Sanmicheli. He began work on the palace in 1556, the same year that the site had been purchased from the Contarini for 9,000 ducats by the procurator Girolamo Grimani. When Sanmicheli died in 1559 the house was still unfinished, though the ground and first floors were nearly complete. The second *piano nobile* was added by the Bergamasque architect Giangiacomo Grigi in the early 1560s and the building was finally completed by Giovanni Antonio Rusconi in 1575. Although the Palazzo Grimani presents a picture of monolithic grandeur, the piecemeal nature of its construction is easily detected. Grigi, for example, was forced to diminish Sanmicheli's *piano nobile* in order that the less generous dimensions of his own addition would not suffer by comparison. If one could visualize Sanmicheli's tall entablature below the *piano nobile* repeated above it and the whole crowned by a heavy projecting cornice, one might conjure up a shadow of Sanmicheli's bold project.

As it is, the first two floors of the house still represent one of the most interesting of Sanmicheli's inventions. The extremely deep-set *piano nobile* windows are handled with a massive simplicity. A single round-arched window lights the side rooms while Sanmicheli's interpretation of the Serlian group of openings lights the *portego* and provides a measured transition between the traditional divisions of a façade. Between these divisions and at the corners, Sanmicheli borrows Coducci's doubled columns from the Vendramin-Calergi. Also from the Vendramin and from earlier Lombard-esque conventions come the pilaster divisions of the ground floor. These exceptionally tall pilasters and all of the façade columns are fluted and all have capitals of the Corinthian type. Such finely carved elements provide the necessary delicacy in a façade where voids and shadows predominate and where the rhythm is based on the massive window unit.

The ground floor is particularly interesting. The tapering of the site towards the back forced Sanmicheli to build the staircase to the *piano nobile* not at right angles to the *andron*, as was traditional, but parallel with it. The *andron* itself is very tall and the architect introduced a series of false groin-vaults on corbels to break up the walls. The water-entrance to the palace is through a triple-arched gate, leading to an atrium, which precedes the *andron* proper. The atrium, the most Roman High Renaissance feature of the entire

105. The Palazzo Grimani, begun by Michele Sanmicheli in 1556, seen from Palazzo Papadopoli

104. An engraving of the ground floor plan of Palazzo Grimani (Cicognara, British Museum)

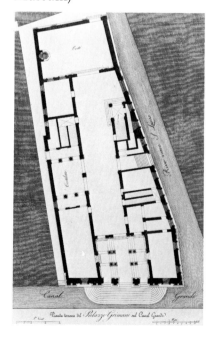

palace, is a full architectural rendering of the Serlian motif that Sanmicheli used as an embellishment in his remodelling of the *andron* at Palazzo Corner-Spinelli. The coffered, barrel-vaulted centre aisle, divided from the flat-ceilinged side aisles by columns, is a motif Sanmicheli may have been familiar with in Rome: the atrium entrance to the Palazzo Farnese by Antonio da Sangallo the Younger is strikingly similar.

At first glance the Palazzo Grimani seems unique in Venice, both in terms of its size and in the boldness of its classicism, but features such as the triple water-

106. OVERLEAF LEFT The ballroom of Palazzo Martinengo

107. OVERLEAF RIGHT The façade of Palazzo Dario at night

171

Palazzo Grimani

gate and the Serlian group of windows with square openings above the flanking lights were copied by a number of later architects. The Palazzo Papadopoli by Grigi, the Palazzo Mocenigo Nero, sometimes attributed to Alessandro Vittoria, and the Palazzo Giustiniani Lolin by Baldassare Longhena are examples of houses in which a modified version of Sanmicheli's Serlian windows appear in the sixteenth and seventeenth centuries. But beyond the popularity of this particular motif, the Palazzo Grimani cannot be said to have been as influential as were the works of Sansovino in contributing to the vocabulary of Venetian palace architecture.

The Venetians found the Palazzo Grimani so impressive that it was rumoured to have cost the colossal sum of 200,000 gold ducats. Certainly the Grimani-Luca, as they were known from their parish, were very rich, and Girolamo, who had the house built, was an important figure in the government of the day. He had been chief of the Council of Ten, four times an ambassador, and a knight of San Marco as well as a procurator. He missed being elected doge by only three votes. But in 1595 his son Marino realized his father's ambition, though his eminence was somewhat eclipsed by the splendour of his wife's role as dogaressa. A doge's coronation was according to tradition an essentially simple affair: after swearing to uphold the constitution and laws of the Republic, he received the ducal *cornù* or cap at the head of the Giant's Staircase in the Palazzo Ducale and then went to the palatine chapel, where he was shown to the populace, standing in the ambo on the right of the iconostasis. Mass was celebrated and afterwards gold coins stamped with the new doge's effigy were scattered to the crowds. Then he retired again to the business of government. By the time of Marino Grimani's election, the doge's wife had become the centre of more elaborate processions and celebrations; those of Dogaressa Morosina Grimani have been recorded in numerous paintings and eye-witness accounts. First she swore to the *promissione ducale*, a list of promises drawn up by a commission on the preceding doge's death and designed to prevent the abuse of ducal power and influence. The Dogaressa Morosina took this oath in the Palazzo Grimani, and after passing under a specially constructed triumphal arch, she boarded a state barge, accompanied, it was said, by two hundred maidens in white silk decorated with gold and silver ornament, an equal number of lavishly costumed matrons, and personally attended by the wives of four procurators. She was rowed to the ducal palace and her arrival there marked the opening of a series of receptions and sumptuous festivities at the new doge's expense. Later governments of the Republic reacted against the extravagance of these festivities, and sumptuary laws were enacted to avoid their repetition. But at the time, Dogaressa Morosina's coronation created such a sensation throughout Italy that Pope Clement VIII was moved to send her the Golden Rose, which on her death bed she bequeathed to the treasury of the palatine chapel, the Basilica of San Marco. The Palazzo Grimani was sold in 1807 to the Municipality of Venice and converted for use as the Central Post Office. Today it houses the Court of Appeal.

Palazzo Corner della Ca' Grande

Before he died in 1527, Giorgio Corner, knight and procurator of San Marco and brother of Queen Caterina Corner of Cyprus, divided his stupendous wealth among four of his five surviving sons. Three of these established separate and important branches of the family. Girolamo inherited the palace his aunt had been born in at San Cassiano; Giovanni settled first at Sant' Angelo (Palazzo Corner-Spinelli) and then in the enormous palace built for him by Sanmicheli at San Polo; eventually Jacopo's descendants inherited the great Gothic palace at San Maurizio, bought by Giorgio from the Malombra family for 20,000 gold ducats and restored at the cost of a further 10,000 ducats. In 1532 a fire broke out in the Palazzo Malombra-Corner, caused by burning coals that had been left smouldering during the night to dry a shipment of sugar from Cyprus. Marin Sanudo, who witnessed the conflagration at San Maurizio, wrote that when it was put out, only a few columns of the *riva* entrance remained. Owing to the complicated and protracted settlement of Giorgio's immense estate, the new palace to be built on the devastated site was probably not begun until 1545. The Ca' Grande, or Great House as it came to be known, was still not quite finished after some three and a half decades of building activity.

The Palazzo Corner della Ca' Grande is remarkable, not for the wealth expended on it or even contained within it, but rather for the quality of its architecture. It is undoubtedly the finest of Jacopo Sansovino's palaces and, what is more significant for the history of Venetian architecture, it is the link between Coducci's great Palazzo Vendramin-Calergi and the immense Baroque creations of Baldassare Longhena. It is also an exceptionally handsome and impressive building. Its tall rectangular proportions recall Coducci's Palazzo Vendramin-Calergi as does the strength of its horizontal divisions. The double columns used in adjusted intervals to make a measured arcade of the tripartite façade are also Codussian. The rest is Sansovino's invention and the whole represents not only the introduction of novel elements into the Venetian architectural vocabulary, but also the first confident adaptation of Roman and Tuscan High Renaissance style to Venetian traditions and conditions.

The rustication of the *pietra d'Istria* at the ground floor is much bolder than Coducci's use of this essentially Tuscan motif at the Corner-Spinelli. The large rusticated voussoirs and keystones of the triple-arched water entrance were part of the Roman and Tuscan idiom of the day. The brackets that frame the mezzanine windows, rather than supporting the entablature above, were

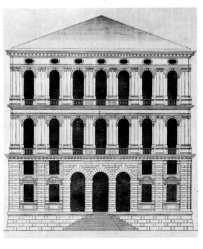

108. An engraving of the façade of Palazzo Corner della Ca' Grande (Cicognara, British Museum)

175

derived from Michelangelo's treatment of the ground-floor windows of the Palazzo Medici. On the upper floors, the projecting box-like balconies inserted between the window columns may have been taken from Raphael's house in Rome, but there need have been no direct derivation as the motif was already widespread and popular. Jacopo Sansovino's training as a sculptor in Florence under Andrea Sansovino, from whom he took his name, is displayed in the spandrel figures and trophies, a decorative motif he had used with even greater richness and variety at the Libreria. In fact, the Palazzo Corner, like the Palazzo Dolfin, seems very sober when compared with the sculpturesque exuberance of Sansovino's public buildings. This is even more evident in the frieze, where the oval windows of the Libreria are repeated, but without the putti, garlands, and elaborate frames that make the Libreria attic so lively.

That Sansovino's private patrons may have required of him a classical *gravitas* is evident not only in the façades of the villa he built for the Garzoni, or the palace at the Rialto for the Dolfin, but especially in the courtyard of the Palazzo Corner. Here rusticated Doric pilasters support a Doric frieze correctly measured with metopes and triglyphs. In the upper floors of the courtyard, the restricted building space available, even to Venetians as rich as the Corner, forces a typically Venetian compromise with the richness of the Tuscan or Roman loggia – the proper Ionic and Corinthian orders are suggested rather than stated and space-saving pilasters are employed rather than columns. However, it is probable that another hand finished the upper floors, so their apparent economies may not have been in keeping with Sansovino's original intentions.

The interior of the Ca' Grande has kept the outlines of the magnificence Sansovino designed for it. But over the years the impressive collections of paintings have been dispersed and virtually nothing is left of that *camera d'oro*, or golden room, which astonished even the most blasé patricians. The caryatids of the giant Sansovinesque chimney were gilded, the walls were hung with cloth of gold, and the cornice of the room was gilded at a cost of 18,000 sequins. The Corner lived on in this house after the fall of the Republic in somewhat diminished splendour, and in 1812 it was sold by the last of his line, Andrea, to the Austrian Government to house the Imperial and Royal Provincial Delegation. In 1817, a fire broke out in the house and the first of a number of extensive restorations resulted. In 1824, the handsome well-head was removed from the courtyard to the campo SS. Giovanni e Paolo, where it can be seen to this day. After the Unification of Italy, the Palazzo Corner became the seat of the Prefect of Venice and in 1932–4 it underwent yet another series of necessary restorations. Today it still houses the Prefecture and, as the seat of the central government's principal representative, it is well maintained.

109. Palazzo Corner della Ca' Grande seen from the water-entrance terrace of Palazzo Venier dei Leoni

110. OVERLEAF LEFT Palazzo Corner della Ca' Grande seen from the roof of the Palazzo Dario

111. OVERLEAF RIGHT Palazzo Corner della Ca' Grande

Palazzo Dolfin-Manin

In 1538 work was begun in the parish of San Salvador on a palace for Giovanni Dolfin, who planned a large house which would incorporate neighbouring property and also, with the government's permission, would be extended over the *fondamenta* on the Grand Canal. By 1540 the façade was completed. The architect of the Palazzo Dolfin, now commonly known as the Palazzo Manin, was Jacopo Sansovino. Since 1529, two years after his arrival in Venice, Sansovino had been protomagister of San Marco, a kind of superintendent of works to the Republic. At the time he was working for the Dolfin at Rialto, he carried out some of the most important commissions of his career, buildings that were to change the face of Venice and make him her most important and influential architect. The Marcian Library in the Piazzetta, the Zecca or Mint on the *molo*, and the Loggetta at the base of the Campanile were all being built at this time. They show Sansovino at his most inventive while displaying his mastery of classical elements enriched with the results of his training as a sculptor. Palazzo Dolfin is a sober exercise in comparison, more closely related to the magnificent classical severity of the Villa Garzoni at Pontecasale than to any of the elaborately sculpturesque public buildings of the Piazza. The courtyard Sansovino designed for the house was a striking innovation in Venice and well illustrated his mastery of the classical vocabulary. Unlike the enclosure of tall brick walls at the back of a Gothic palace, this courtyard was incorporated in the palace itself and like the one he built at the Palazzo Corner della Ca' Grande, its walls were correctly ordered with Doric, Ionic and Corinthian pilasters.

On the façade, the open arcade of the ground floor, in some ways the Palazzo Dolfin's most distinctive feature, is not, as has so often been claimed, an example of Sansovino's inventiveness, but shows his handsome treatment of a traditional feature of a Venetian palace extended over a public walkway. An example of the Veneto-Byzantine period exists at the Falier house at SS. Apostoli and of the Gothic period at the Palazzo Barbaro, as well as numerous other *sottoporteghi* scattered throughout the city. The arcade of the *sottoportego* at the Palazzo Dolfin-Manin is faced with Doric pilasters and the floors above with Ionic and Corinthian half-columns. The upper orders are disposed at intervals, recalling Coducci's attempts to make of the Venetian tripartite façade a regular arcade. Sansovino's plain frieze, decorated only with lion's heads, further shows his debt to local tradition and more specifically to the rhythms of Coducci's friezes at the Palazzo Corner-Spinelli and the Vendramin-Calergi.

Giorgio Vasari in his life of Sansovino says that the house cost Giovanni

112. The façade of Palazzo Dolfin-Manin

Dolfin some 30,000 ducats. During the years they lived here the Dolfin of San Salvador were known as 'of the Ca' Grande'. They claimed an ancestor who was bishop of Aquileia in 434, one doge, five cardinals, and numerous important generals and high officials of the Republic. The lighter side of their family history is represented by their patronage at San Salvador of a *compagnia delle calze* known as the *Accessi,* a pun falling somewhere between those 'admitted' and those 'having a fit'. The *calze* were clubs of young nobles under twenty-six who amused themselves, before joining the ranks of the Great Council, with parties, pranks, and a general display of anything other than their elders' *gravitas*. They, their valets and their gondoliers wore particoloured hose which identified the company they belonged to; their colourful costume and youthful posturing made them natural subjects for the painters of the day. Carpaccio depicted them in several paintings now in the Accademia Gallery. Among the many entertainments devised by the *compagnie delle calze* in sixteenth-century Venice were performances of classical plays and comedies in the contemporary dialect. The names of Aretino and Vasari are linked with particularly lavish productions at Palazzo Dolfin and in 1565 Andrea Palladio was commissioned to build a wooden theatre on classical lines in the courtyard of the house.

When the Dolfin della Ca' Grande died out in 1602, the Palazzo Dolfin was divided among a number of heirs and, for a time, was partitioned to accommodate the different families who laid claim to the estate. Among the heirs were members of the Contarini degli Scrigni and a branch of the Pesaro. From these last the palace was bought some time after 1789 by a Pesaro kinsman, the last doge, Lodovico Manin. Manin has been much maligned by

Palazzo Dolfin-Manin

historians of the Republic. The truth is that he was a mediocre man who reached the ducal dignity by making no enemies (he held no influential offices before his election) and by being extremely rich, even according to the inflated standards of the eighteenth century. He carried out ceremonial duties, such as accompanying Pope Pius VI through the Veneto, with magnificent largesse and he bore the cost of the ducal election with nonchalance. In his will he left a legacy of 100,000 ducats to the orphans of San Servolo. At the Palazzo Dolfin, he commissioned Giovanni Antonio Selva, the architect of the Fenice theatre, to enlarge, remodel, and redecorate the house. Happily, Selva's plan to remodel the façade was never carried out, nor was the building extended all the way to the campo San Salvador as he had intended. But the interior was redecorated and Sansovino's courtyard was altered beyond recognition. In accordance with the taste of the time a large collection of casts of classical statuary was put together to decorate the principal hall.

The Manin family were recent arrivals in Venice though they had long played an important role in the aristocracy of the Veneto. They had come to Udine in the Friuli from Tuscany as a result of the Guelf and Ghibelline struggles of the early fourteenth century. Like many of the Friulian Veneto families they frequently owed allegiance both to the Republic and to the Holy Roman Emperor. One of Lodovico's ancestors was knighted by Charles V. But the wars of the Republic against the Turk gave many of these families the chance to join the exclusive Venetian patriciate; a contribution to the war effort of 60,000 ducats secured the Manin their place in the Golden Book. Once established in Venice, their riches and generosity were striking; in 1728 they paid for the building of the extravagant Gesuiti church (Santa Maria Assunta) as well as for an elaborate family chapel at the church of the discalced Carmelites.

Despite his spineless and melancholy abdication of the millennial ducal dignity, Lodovico Manin cannot be blamed for Napoleon's destruction of the Republic. Napoleon himself, writing in exile at Saint Helena, pointed to the one Venetian he considered responsible, and it is indeed arguable that had Manin's kinsman, ambassador Francesco Pesaro, accepted the Corsican general's offer of alliance against the Austrians, the Republic might have survived – but for how long is another question. On political grounds alone – not to mention the financial, commercial, and military weaknesses of Venice in 1796–7 – it is doubtful that it could have remained immune to the revolutionary fervour of Directoire France, or to the equally alien spirit of totalitarianism embodied in the Napoleonic empire, or to the subsequent Metternichian reaction. The traditional moderation and conservatism of the Serene Republic had no place in the Europe of Bonapartism and its aftermath.

After his abdication, Manin lived for a time with the Grimani at Santa Fosca and then with the Pesaro at San Stae. He returned to his house in 1801 and died there shortly afterwards. The house changed hands many times in the nineteenth century and recently it has been adapted, after extensive and for the most part careful restoration, as the headquarters of the Banca d' Italia.

Palazzo Papadopoli

The Palazzo Papadopoli at Sant' Aponal was built for the Coccina family in the early 1560s by Giangiacomo Grigi of Bergamo. This architect supervised the completion of the Scuola di San Rocco and added the second floor to Sanmicheli's great Palazzo Grimani, which stood opposite the Coccina house on the Grand Canal. At the Palazzo Papadopoli he created a type of Venetian façade which retained its appeal to the essential conservatism of the Venetian patriciate throughout the period of Baroque extravagance until the neo-classical revival. If Sansovino's Palazzo Corner is the link between Coducci's Vendramin-Calergi and the heavy Baroque of the Rezzonico and Pesaro palaces, Grigi's Palazzo Papadopoli is the link between the classicizing Lombardesque of the Contarini-Polignac and Contarini-Figure and such palaces as the Balbi, the Mocenigo Nero, Longhena's Giustiniani-Lolin, Massari's Palazzo Grassi and Visentini's façade for the Palazzo Valmarana-Mangilli at SS. Apostoli.

The fine proportions of the house have long been acknowledged and at various times it has been attributed to Alessandro Vittoria for its similarity to the façade of the Palazzo Balbi and even to Palladio for the purity and harmony of its proportions. Unlike the masterpieces of Coducci, Sansovino, or Sanmicheli, the walls are hardly broken up by windows; the tripartite divisions of the traditional palace façade are not disguised, and pilasters are used instead of columns. A prominent role is given to carved decorative elements such as coats of arms, cartouches, and raised rectangular plaques, which help relieve the flatness of the façade wall.

The *portego* windows at the Palazzo Papadopoli are composed in the Serlian group derived from Sanmicheli's Palazzo Grimani: small square windows are placed above the lower side windows. The windows of the side rooms are upright rectangles surmounted by segmented and triangular pediments as at Sanmicheli's Palazzo Gussoni. The attic frieze adopts Sansovino's oval windows from the Libreria and the Palazzo Corner and is treated in the simplest way.

The Coccina family, who commissioned the palace and who lived here until they died out in 1748, were dealers in jewels and had come from Bergamo to establish themselves in Venice in the sixteenth century. They belonged to the citizen class of the Republic, but seemed more interested in mercantile ventures than in service to the State. They were, however, considerable patrons of the arts and in about 1571 commissioned four canvases from Paolo Veronese to decorate a room in the house. On the two long walls

113. An engraving of the façade of Palazzo Papadopoli (Visentini, *Venetian Palaces,* I, British Museum)

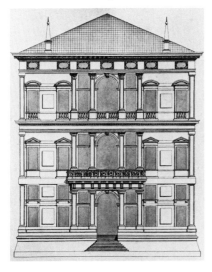

were placed *The Marriage at Cana* and, opposite, *The Adoration of the Magi*. One of the short walls held a *Christ on the Road to Calvary*, while opposite hung a splendid votive picture showing Zuanbattista Coccina, his wife, brothers and children presented to the Virgin by their patron saints, with figures of various Virtues. In the background behind one of the children Paolo depicted Grigi's façade of the family palace on the Grand Canal. All four canvases are now in Dresden.

The palace was bought from the Coccina estate by a branch of the ancient Tiepolo family, descendants of a Roman consular *gens* who had governed in Rimini and then fled from the barbarians to the safety of the lagoon. The Tiepolo gave two doges to Venice in the thirteenth century and the infamous Bajamonte Tiepolo, who conspired with the Querini to overthrow the republican government and install a monarchy in his own person. The plot was thwarted, the houses of that branch of the family at San Stin nearby were razed to the ground and a column of infamy planted on the site as a perpetual reminder of their attempted treachery to the sovereign idea of the State. The Tiepolo who bought the Palazzo Papadopoli in the early eighteenth century had innumerable illustrious forebears, including a Patriarch of Venice in 1619. The last of the Sant' Aponal line was G. Domenico Tiepolo, a historian of Venice, whose heirs sold the house to one Valentino Comello. Then it changed hands several times until the Papadopoli bought it in 1864. They, like the Calergi of an earlier epoch, were from Candia in Crete; they had established themselves in Venice in the eighteenth century and their riches were proverbial. In 1874–5 they demolished the buildings to the left of the house to create a canal-side garden and they added the immense wings behind. At the same time they employed the antiquarian, Michelangelo Gugenheim, to redecorate the interior, which he did with a lavishness and attention to detail that is impressive even today though its nineteenth-century origins are sometimes painfully obvious. The palace today houses part of the complex of the University of Venice as well as the National Research Institute for the Movement of Grand Masses – a scientific laboratory concerned with geology and oceanography which has carried out important investigations concerning the sinking of the city and the apparent increased frequency of the *acque alte*, or high tides.

114. The façade of Palazzo Papadopoli, completed in the 1560s by Giangiacomo Grigi

Palazzo Balbi

The Palazzo Balbi is hardly ever identified with its parish of San Pantalon, but is known rather by its position at the *volta del canal*. Its situation and its architecture make it one of the most prominent of all Venetian palaces, especially in the iconography of the Grand Canal. The eighteenth-century view painters depicted it often, either as the focal point of the sweep of the canal from the Carità (now the Accademia) or else as the foreground for the stretch of the canal to Rialto; together with the Palazzo Foscari it is today the subject of countless postcards. The architect obviously gave great consideration to its position, and its dimensions suggest that he purposely designed it as a pendant to the great fifteenth-century palace of the Foscari. The Palazzo Balbi has been attributed to Alessandro Vittoria and there seems little reason to doubt that a master of his talents – and especially his sense of the theatrical – created this masterpiece of Venetian scenography. His patron, too, seems to have given great importance to the effect it created when seen from the canal, for it is said that he and his family lived on an elaborately furnished and decorated barge moored across from the site while the palace was being built.

The Balbi palace was built between 1582 and 1590 and is based on the type established by Giangiacomo Grigi at the Palazzo Papadopoli. That is to say that wall space predominates and the tripartite division of the Venetian façade is not disguised. The façade remains a two-dimensional surface onto which decorative elements are laid. The pilasters which divide the two *piani nobili* into three compartments are perhaps derived from such transitional Lombardesque palaces as the Contarini delle Figure and the Contarini-Polignac. But at the Palazzo Balbi these pilasters are doubled, just as the simpler, classically segmented and triangular pediments of the Palazzo Papadopoli are here opened, with ornamental finials standing in the openings. These elaborations are mannerist in spirit as is the treatment of the *portego* group of windows. Instead of the Papadopoli's Serlian motif, the architect has used three traditional round-arched windows, but has given them a strikingly mannerist feeling by separating them with double Ionic columns. However mannerist or proto-Baroque the façade may seem, its individual elements could be derived from earlier traditions: not only the Lombardesque use of pilasters and wall space, or the Codussian rustication of the ground floor, or the Sansovinesque attic windows, but also the mannerist doubled columns separating round-arched windows vaguely recall the Veneto-Byzantine palace arcades. The purely mannerist elements which were later taken up by Baroque artists were the open pediments, the elaborately carved arms, cartouches, and sculpturesque window frames.

115. Palazzo Balbi, built between 1582 and 1590 by Alessandro Vittoria

187

Palazzo Balbi

The Balbi of the *volta del canal* claimed descent from the ancient *gens* Balba who, according to Tacitus, had come to Rome from Spain. The family reached Venice by the usual slow stages, settling in earlier times at Pavia, Milan, and finally Ravenna. In Venice they proliferated into thirteen branches and members of the San Pantalon branch became famous for their learned pursuits. One Luigi Balbi established an extensive library and music studio at the Palazzo Balbi; Gasparo was a celebrated cosmographer and traveller; and Adriano, in the late eighteenth century, was a well-known geographer. In 1737 Lorenzo Balbi spent over a thousand ducats on remodelling the house and commissioned the busts of twelve Greek philosophers to decorate the *portego*.

But the learned accomplishments of the Balbi are now mostly forgotten and in the popular imagination the Palazzo Balbi is more often associated with the conqueror of Venice. It was from the balcony of this house that Napoleon watched the regatta staged in his honour on 2 December 1807. The Venetian regatta now takes place annually, but in Napoleon's day, and indeed since the first regatta in 1315, the colourful and elaborate parade of ceremonial barges,

116. The *volta del canal*, with a section of the Giustinian and Foscari houses on the left, and Palazzo Moro-Lin on the right framing Palazzo Balbi and Palazzo Civran-Grimani

117. Detail of the *portego* balcony of Palazzo Balbi

followed by a gondola race, was staged only during state visits or as a signal honour to a visiting dignitary. The finishing line for the races was then as now in front of the Palazzo Balbi, where the judges and other dignitaries were seated on an elaborately canopied float called *la Machina* (The Machine). The best artists of the day made designs for the Machina and for the ambassadors' ornate twelve-oared barges. Designs for such boats by Tiepolo and Guardi still survive and the eighteenth-century regattas with the Palazzo Balbi in the left foreground are still the best known to us through the paintings of Carlevaris and Canaletto.

Napoleon's visit to the Palazzo Balbi was to be commemorated with a plaque inscribed to *Magnus Napoleon*, but the gesture was never carried out. In the mid-nineteenth century the palace was owned by the antiquary Michelangelo Gugenheim, who attempted to revive Venetian crafts. Laboratories and workshops were installed in the house, but had to be closed in 1900. In 1913 Gugenheim put his collections up for auction and in 1925 the house was bought by the Adriatic Electricity Company. In 1973 it became the seat of the regional government of the Veneto and underwent extensive restoration.

Palazzo Mocenigo

The Mocenigo palaces at San Samuel have often confused visitors to Venice. In some guidebooks they are said to be three in number and in others four; the Mocenigo Vecchio, which gives its name to a *calle*, is confused with the house called the Palazzo Nero; and the famous inhabitants of the various houses are often located in the wrong ones. There are four Mocenigo palaces, but the central two are actually a double palace, originally meant to be lived in as one house. The oldest, the Mocenigo Vecchio, stands nearest the *volta del canal*. In the late sixteenth century the Palazzo Nero was built two houses away, towards the Rialto, and in the eighteenth century a double palace was built between these two, not to connect them, but to enlarge the Palazzo Nero, with whose floors its own correspond.

The *casa vecchia*, the oldest of the four houses, was originally a Gothic building as can still be seen from architectural details surviving on the garden side. The foundations are supposed to be very ancient, but the seventeenth-

118. The Mocenigo arms from the eighteenth-century double Mocenigo palace

119. Palazzo Mocenigo-Nero, the late sixteenth-century 'new' house

century remodelling has obliterated all indications of what the original building looked like. Presumably one of the oldest branches of the family first settled here; these Mocenigo had come from Milan and were thought to be descendants of the Cornelii of Rome. They provided seven doges to the Republic – only one less than the Contarini. The reign of Alvise I Mocenigo saw the great victory over the Turks at Lepanto, the building of the Redentore church – the trowel with which the doge laid the cornerstone is still kept in the house – and the celebrated visit of King Henry III of France to Venice. The Mocenigo gave hospitality to Emmanuele Philiberto, Duke of Savoy, during the king's visit, a fact recorded on a plaque on the *casa vecchia* façade. In 1591–2 Giovanni Mocenigo of the *casa vecchia* branch (the new house being complete and a separate branch of the family already associated with it) invited the controversial philosopher-monk Giordano Bruno to live in the house as his guest. Bruno stayed for almost eight months but failed to reveal to his host the secrets of alchemy and magic Mocenigo supposed him to have. Disappointed, frustrated, and angered, Mocenigo denounced him to the Venetian Inquisition on rather obscure grounds. The Inquisitors of Venice were not, as their name might imply, primarily concerned with religious matters, but rather with treason and public morality. None the less a great deal of pressure was put on them by the Roman Holy Office to release Bruno to the pope for examination on the grounds of heresy. Despite the implicit infringement of Venetian sovereignty, the Senate voted to turn him over to Rome, where for seven years he was examined according to sixteenth-century methods. He was tortured, found guilty of heretical teaching, and burned at the stake on the Campo dei Fiori in February 1600. His ghost is said to haunt the house of his host and betrayer to this day.

In the sixteenth century the Mocenigo bought from the Bembo a property which became the seat of the *casa nuova* branch of the family. The Palazzo Nero was built around 1579 and is sometimes attributed to Alessandro Vittoria. Its plain *pietra d'Istria* front with Serlian *portego* windows and pedimented lateral windows is an almost exact copy of the Palazzo Papadopoli's façade. It was from this house that the painted allegorical friezes, portraits, and handsome sixteenth-century ceilings *alla Sansovino* were removed to decorate the simpler rooms of the later double palace. In 1621 Anne, Countess of Arundel, hired apartments here and inadvertently became embroiled in the politics of the day. A former Venetian ambassador to England, Antonio Foscarini, had been denounced to the Council of Ten for treason. He was secretly tried and executed, and his body was displayed between the two columns in the Piazzetta to the considerable consternation of the populace. Rumours spread that he had had forbidden and possibly treasonable conversations with the Countess of Arundel. In high dudgeon the indomitable Englishwoman sought redress from both the Senate and the doge himself, and an official investigation was ordered forthwith. It emerged that the denunciation of Foscarini came from an envious political subordinate and that Lady Arundel was innocent of any involvement. The Council of Ten was forced to confess its error in public and Foscarini's body was exhumed and given a State burial with full honours while the doge personally read a solemn declaration of apology to Lady Arundel.

In the early eighteenth century the double Mocenigo palace was joined to the Palazzo Nero. The double palace does not have particularly distinguished architecture, but the lion's heads and Mocenigo rosettes are well employed as a decorative motif in the spandrels of the plain Serlian window frames. These houses, too, were famous in Venice for their English associations. In the eighteenth century Lady Mary Wortley Montagu hired apartments here during one of her visits to Venice and bedevilled the British consul of the day, Canaletto's patron Joseph Smith, as much as Lady Arundel had pestered the British ambassador Sir Henry Wotton a century earlier.

But the double Mocenigo house is most often associated in the English visitor's mind with Lord Byron, who lived there in 1818–19. It was here that his tempestuous mistress, Margarita Cogni (a baker's wife and hence known as La Fornarina), held sway, that he wrote the first two cantos of *Don Juan*, that he was visited by the censorious Shelley and that he met the eighteen-year-old contessa from Ravenna, Teresa Guiccioli. He has given us, in some of his letters, a glimpse of his life in the Mocenigo: of his fourteen servants, his

120. Palazzo Mocenigo, hired by Lord Byron from 1817 to 1819

valet and his gondolier, of the billiard-table he set up in one of the *portego* rooms, and of the menagerie of dogs, birds, and a fox that lived with him. He kept his carriage in the *andron*, but makes no mention of the giant statue that is still to be found there, an over-lifesize marble statue of Napoleon, half-dressed in a Roman toga and with his arm extended in a Roman salute. It was intended to stand in the centre of the Napoleonic wing of the Piazza, flanked by statues of the twelve Caesars, but somehow the order got muddled and it was delivered to the Mocenigo family instead.

In the later nineteenth century the Mocenigo made marriages with Austrian families and secured for themselves a role in the development of various Venetian industries. They helped introduce the *vaporetti*, or water-bus service in the lagoon, which later plied the Grand Canal. The *casa vecchia* passed out of the hands of the Mocenigo on the extinction of that branch in 1868, but the double palace and the Palazzo Nero were still joined together and inhabited by the Mocenigo and their descendants until the last war. After the war, the houses were separated and though the descendants of the family still live in part of the double palace the rest has been divided and sold as apartments.

121. The Grand Canal with (from left to right) Palazzo Mocenigo-Nero, the double Mocenigo palace, Palazzo Mocenigo Vecchio, Palazzo Contarini delle Figure and the twin Giustinian palace

Palazzo Donà delle Rose

The Palazzo Donà delle Rose at the Fondamenta Nuove is one of the very few palaces in Venice still inhabited by descendants of the family for whom it was built. It is also the only palace included in this study that is situated in the northern part of the island. The fondamenta nuove, or quay-like promenade, antedates the palace itself and probably determined its siting. From the outside, its principal façade overlooks the rio dei Gesuiti, yet the axis of the interior is made by the *portego* and *andron*, which run the length of the palace to the fondamenta. The façades are very plain and flat, reminiscent of those that were intended to receive fresco decoration. The only architectural feature of note is the Serlian window adapted from the Palazzo Papadopoli and here placed in the centre of the rio façade as well as in the centre of the fondamenta façade.

122. Detail of an engraving of Palazzo Donà delle Rose showing the Serlian windows

Apart from its curious plan, its position, and its association with a single family of an otherwise highly mobile patriciate, the Palazzo Donà is interesting for its link with one of the extraordinary personalities of Venetian history. Its cornerstone was laid on 24 March 1610 by the doge Leonardo Donà, whose political career is in some ways typical of the talented patrician who late in life achieved the ducal dignity. At the age of twenty he gained his first experience of Venetian administration in Cyprus. At thirty-four he was sent as ambassador to Spain and six years later he was elected a Savio of the doge's council. From then on he was employed on various embassies and served two years as Podestà of Brescia. He was ambassador to six popes and at fifty-five was elected a procurator di San Marco. Later still he became *provveditor* for Friuli and then for the whole of the mainland. At the age of seventy he was elected doge and he died six years later. His brief reign is one of the most significant in Venetian history because during it he successfully defended Venice's liberty and sovereignty.

The threat came from papal Rome and at first hinged on a technicality of legal jurisdiction. Both sides remained intransigent, each insisting on its rights; the impasse was broken with Paul V's condemnation of the Venetian Republic. The Senate was excommunicated and the Republic was placed under an interdict. Donà employed countermeasures such as preventing the publication of the Bull of excommunication and threatening priests disloyal to the Republic with arrest. Through complicated diplomatic manoeuvres a compromise was reached and the papal ban was lifted. Donà had successfully preserved the sovereign integrity of Venice. In the struggle with Rome, he was helped by his theological adviser Paolo Sarpi, a Servite monk who was

Palazzo Donà delle Rose

arguably the most original thinker Venice ever produced. Fra Paolo survived assassination attempts instigated by his enemies in Rome and, like his master, was hard at work for the Republic until the day he died. Given his talents and his close association with the doge it is hardly surprising that the talented Sarpi is often spoken of as the architect of the Donà delle Rose palace. But extant documents make clear that the palace was never finished according to the original plans. It seems that this was partly due to the doge's brother Nicolò, whose interference was so effective that the doge is said to have died of apoplexy after one of their arguments about the building.

123. Palazzo Donà delle Rose at Fondamenta Nuove – the fondamenta façade

BAROQUE PALACES

Palazzo Giustiniani-Lolin

The Palazzo Giustiniani-Lolin near the Academy bridge in the parish of San Vidal introduces the work of Venice's greatest Baroque architect, Baldassare Longhena. The palace is a youthful work, probably completed by 1623 when Giovanni Lolin, for whom it had been built, left it to his daughter Francesca, who had married a member of the Giustinian family. The young Longhena trained under the architect and theoretician Vincenzo Scamozzi, a disciple of Palladio, and it is in this building that the classical restraint of his training is most evident. But no matter how exuberant his later creations became in comparison with the house he built for the Lolin, Longhena's dependence on the traditions of Venetian architecture is always evident. At the Palazzo Giustiniani-Lolin, he follows the conservative interpretation of Sanmicheli's Serlian motif as used by Grigi in the Palazzo Papadopoli over half a century earlier. The treatment of the *portego* window groups is almost identical: in both cases the three elements of the Serlian window are separated by tall pilasters. The large area of wall space between the lateral windows is relieved with raised squares of *pietra d'Istria*. The balconies are suppressed, with the exception of the *piano nobile portego* balcony, which projects. What is distinctively Longhena's at the Giustiniani-Lolin is the use of round-arched lateral windows with keystone heads instead of rectangular windows surmounted by pediments. In other respects the house corresponds in most details to the type of the Papadopoli and Mocenigo-Nero palaces.

The sculpturism which became such a hallmark of Longhena's work is hardly evident at all save for the neatly carved draperies looped like garlands between the capitals of the second *piano nobile* pilasters, a derivation from Grapiglia's façade for the Palazzo Loredan in the nearby Campo Santo Stefano. And the use of a conservative Codussian rustication on the ground floor gives no hint of the cyclopean *pietra d'Istria* blocks that Longhena was to use at the Pesaro and Rezzonico houses. It was only some years after the Palazzo Giustinian-Lolin was built that he received the commission to build the great, and architecturally unique, Baroque votive church dedicated to Santa Maria della Salute. This great invention, which has become so much a part of the Venetian landscape, has elements that derive from Longhena's training under Palladio's disciple, but the whole is so sculpturesque in feeling and so endlessly elaborated that something of his later distinctive style of palace building may be linked to it.

A branch of the Giustinian family lived in the house until the early nineteenth century. In 1864, the last duchess of Parma, the Regent Luisa

124. Palazzo Giustiniani-Lolin, completed by Baldassare Longhena in 1623

Maria, died in apartments she had rented here. In 1880 the house underwent a typically heavy-handed nineteenth-century restoration; and recently the last private owners, Ugo and Olga Levi, have bequeathed their impressive collection of music manuscripts and their library to the city and a centre for musical studies has been established in their house.

125. Longhena's use of plain, flat Istrian stone decoration at Palazzo Giustiniani-Lolin

Palazzo Belloni-Battagia

The Palazzo Belloni-Battagia was built by Baldassare Longhena between 1647 and 1663 for Girolamo Belloni. It is the second of the four houses by Longhena included in this study and marks the transition from the restrained conventions of the Palazzo Giustiniani-Lolin to the full-blown Baroque of the Pesaro and Rezzonico palaces. The wall space of the façade still predominates here, as it does at the Giustiniani-Lolin and its prototype, Giangiacomo Grigi's Palazzo Papadopoli, but Longhena has taken the decorative elements not from those austere examples but from the mannerist treatment of Alessandro Vittoria's Palazzo Balbi. The open pediments are the most obvious examples of this borrowing, though at the Palazzo Belloni they have lost what structural sense they had and are placed on a cornice with dentils that runs across the façade above the round-arched windows of the *piano nobile*. The cornice with its pediments and the heavy-balustered projecting balcony, which also runs the width of the entire façade, make the *piano nobile* a very strongly marked horizontal unit. The windows of the floor are not a Sansovinesque or Codussian single arcade, as they are at the Pesaro and

126. The classical water-gate at Palazzo Belloni-Battagia with handsome grilles and a carved stone base

Rezzonico houses, but are well separated by two highly carved coats of arms placed as prominently as those of the Palazzo Balbi. The water entrance is also reminiscent of the Palazzo Balbi though here it is crowned by a broken instead of an open pediment. The attic floor is treated with the same restraint as at the Giustiniani-Lolin and an even more remarkable throwback is the frieze, which is decorated with well-spaced star and crescent motifs taken from the Belloni arms, providing a conscious echo of the frieze of Loredan achievements on Coducci's Palazzo Vendramin-Calergi, which stands opposite it on the canal.

Girolamo Belloni, who commissioned the palace, did not belong to the ancient family of that name who had settled in Venice in the ninth century; they died out in the fourteenth century. Girolamo paid some 150,000 ducats to ensure his inclusion in the Golden Book in 1648, at the same time as Longhena was constructing his handsome palace. It seems that the cost of his ambitions made heavy inroads on his fortune and by 1663 he was forced to rent his house to Count Czernin, the imperial ambassador to Venice. From Girolamo, the house passed to the family of his daughter's second marriage, the Battagia. They were also recently ennobled, having been admitted to the Great Council in 1500 after Pier Antonio Battagia surrendered the castle of Cremona to the Republic. In 1667 another Battagia was *provveditor* at Candia during its siege by the Turks; he was wounded by a bomb. For all the heroism displayed by the Venetians and by Battagia during the siege, the island still had to be surrendered and he returned in disgrace to Venice. He was tried and imprisoned, but like so many heroes of the Venetian Republic before him, he was finally exonerated of the charge of neglecting his duties and was freed.

In the early nineteenth century the palace was sold to Antonio Capovilla, an industrialist, who radically altered the interior and redecorated it throughout. He kept the busts of the twelve Roman emperors that decorated the *andron*, the rich marble facing of the staircase, and the grisailles by the frescoist Giambattista Canal (1745–1825) done from designs by Tiepolo, whose pupil he was. Later the house changed hands several times and is now divided into offices and apartments.

127. Palazzo Belloni-Battagia, built by Baldassare Longhena between 1647 and 1663

Palazzo Rezzonico

The palace best known to the visitor to Venice is the Palazzo Rezzonico at San Barnaba on the Grand Canal. The Ca' Rezzonico, as it is popularly and correctly called, now houses the city's museum of eighteenth-century decorative arts – a collection of furnishings and art treasures from various Venetian family houses – and gives a partial idea of the patrician splendour of an eighteenth-century Venetian palace. Though the palazzo was completed in the mid-eighteenth century, its architecture is a product of the seventeenth-century Baroque. Baldassare Longhena, who was commissioned by the procurator Filippo Bon to build it on the site of the old Bon houses at San Barnaba, began his work in 1667, about nine years before the Pesaro at San Stae employed him. The building is in many ways more satisfactory than the palace for the Pesaro: whereas the latter has an overwhelming architectural exuberance, Ca' Rezzonico achieves a more classical harmony and balance and thus more accurately reflects the generally conservative building tastes of the patriciate. The solemn *gravitas* of the façade is particularly evident in the rusticated ground floor, the most original part of Longhena's building. Half-columns with the same low-relief rustication as appears on the walls give a movement and strength which provides a strong base for the arcade above. The single large windows in each bay of the ground floor (and from inside their extraordinary size is more striking, for they are practically as tall as the

128. Palazzo Malipiero at San Samuele – a view of the garden and Ca' Rezzonico

129. Palazzo Rezzonico (left) before completion, in a painting by Canaletto

Palazzo Rezzonico

mezzanine rooms themselves) enhance the strong uncluttered effect of the ground-floor façade. The triple water-gate entrance is also treated with the utmost simplicity: the rusticated columns rise to support a flat architrave instead of flanking archways of the type used by Sansovino and his followers. The *piano nobile* is treated in the arcade-like fashion of Sansovino's Palazzo Corner della Ca' Grande, and the window units are derived from there and from Sansovino's Marcian Library; both motifs are repeated at the Palazzo Pesaro, but in a much more extravagant and sculpturesque way.

It was a vastly expensive building and the procurator and his heirs found that they could not afford to finish it. At Longhena's death in 1682 it was complete only to the height of the *piano nobile*. In 1745 the heirs of the procurator, who had died in 1712, hired Giorgio Massari to add the next two floors, but the costs were too great and they were forced to sell the uncompleted building to the extremely rich Rezzonico family in 1750. Gian Battista Rezzonico retained the services of Massari, who brought the palace to completion in 1756.

The Rezzonico were an ancient and noble family from Como, who in the person of Gian Battista and his two brothers had been admitted to the Libro d'Oro in 1687 after donating the practically statutory 100,000 ducats to the Venetian treasury. Two years after the completion of the house, Gian Battista's son Carlo, the Bishop of Padua, was elected Pope and took the name of Clement XIII. He soon became well-known for his nepotism in Rome: he created two of his nephews Cardinals and a third a Roman Senator. The Venetian state, which had traditionally regarded papal ambitions with suspicion, seemed overjoyed by his election. Even though his family had only recently been admitted to the Great Council, the Republic bestowed on all

131. Ca' Rezzonico seen from the balcony of Palazzo Grassi

130. The *piano nobile portego* window group at Palazzo Rezzonico

132. The staircase hall, built at the back of Ca' Rezzonico in the eighteenth century

the Rezzonico the hereditary Knighthood of San Marco – a distinction heretofore held only by the descendants of three of Venice's most ancient families, the Contarini, Morosini, and Querini. When in 1761 the Republic raised one of the pope's nephews to the coveted and profitable dignity of procurator of San Marco, Clement waited only eighteen days before bestowing on the Most Serene Republic the highest honour the papacy could pay to a secular power or individual, the Golden Rose. Besides his nepotism and the riches and power he brought his Venetian family, Papa Rezzonico was known to the great critic and collector J. J. Winckelmann as *Sua Scrupulosità* for the scrupulousness with which his order was carried out to cover the private parts of every statue in the vast Vatican collections with fig-leaves.

In 1769, the year of the pope's death, the splendour of the Rezzonico palace was such that the Republic chose it to stage an elaborate entertainment in honour of Emperor Joseph II. One hundred young girls from four of the city's conservatoires serenaded him until four in the morning. Six hundred patricians were invited and one hundred and twenty richly dressed ladies added to the brilliance of the occasion. However, contemporary accounts indicate that the serious, liberal-minded young emperor preferred his quarters in the Inn of the Leon Bianco to all the magnificent festivities.

133. The throne-room of Ca' Rezzonico

Palazzo Rezzonico

While many documents attest the splendour of the Rezzonico furnishings, it is the plan of the house that is of particular interest. The Palazzo Rezzonico is the first house considered in this study that illustrates the effect of vast riches and Baroque taste on the living patterns of the Venetian patriciate. The vast reception rooms of the *piano nobile* came more and more to be used as state rooms and the mezzanine below was transformed from offices into more intimate living quarters – especially winter apartments. The pope, when he was Bishop of Padua, had his pied-à-terre in the mezzanine of the family palace. The library and archives once housed on this floor were moved to the attics, where a librarian looked after them. The *portego* was not considered grand enough for entertaining and an entire building was added onto the palace in the eighteenth century just to house an immense frescoed ballroom and the grand staircase leading to it. Besides the fresco masterpiece of Giovanni Battista Crosato in the ballroom, the Rezzonico employed the best artists of the day to decorate the rooms of the house. The ceiling panel by Giovanni Battista Tiepolo celebrating the marriage of Ludovico Rezzonico to the Friulian heiress Faustina Savorgnan is still *in situ*.

Despite their riches and grand marriages, the Rezzonico family of San Barnaba died out in 1810. The house changed hands several times in the nineteenth century and was owned at one time by Robert 'Pen' Barrett Browning and his American wife. In 1889, his father came to spend Christmas in the pied-à-terre 'Pen' had prepared for him in the Bishop of Padua's mezzanine. He caught a chill, which developed into pneumonia, and died there on 12 December, the same day his last volume of poems, *Asolando*, appeared in London. The last private owner of the Rezzonico was the Baron Hirschel de Minerbi, from whom Cole Porter hired the principal apartments in the 1920s. In 1931 the palace was bought by the city and in 1936 the present museum was installed and inaugurated.

134. The Rezzonico coat of arms

Palazzo Pesaro

In his will of 1652, Doge Giovanni Pesaro exhorted his family to complete the new palace begun on the site of three houses he had had demolished in the parish of San Stae. He also left some 12,000 ducats for his own funerary monument in the Frari church. In both cases the architect associated with the doge's dispositions was to be Baldassare Longhena. The doge died in 1659 and his tomb took ten years to complete; the doge's heir, the procurator Leonardo Pesaro, retained Longhena to work on the palace and the date carved on the façade, 1679, probably refers to the completion of its sculptural decoration.

The scale the Pesaro had in mind for their house can be seen by the fact that it was begun in the doge's lifetime and the first work was on the courtyard well back from the Grand Canal. It took over fifty-eight years to complete the building as we see it. Longhena's death in 1682 brought the work to a standstill, but it had at least reached the height of the *piano nobile*. His plans were faithfully executed by Antonio Gaspari, who completed the house in 1710, and the architecture of the whole may be said to be Longhena's own. Beside its great size, what is striking about the palace is the rich Baroque idiom of its sculptural mass and decoration. But to the student of Venetian architecture, it is immediately apparent that for all the originality of rich detail, the basic forms are those of Sansovino's Palazzo Corner della Ca' Grande, built over one hundred years earlier. And while Sansovino's palace is cited as Longhena's prototype, an even earlier model, Coducci's palace for the Loredan, must also be remembered.

The Sansovinesque inheritance of the Palazzo Pesaro is particularly obvious in the *piano nobile*, where Longhena adopts the arcade-like motif of columns and window intervals to disguise the tripartite conventions of the traditional Venetian palace façade. The elaborate windows he uses are a direct borrowing from Sansovino's Library, but the doubling of the columns at the ends of the building and between the lateral and *portego* windows is adapted from Coducci. The broad, semicircular sweep of steps from the water to the water-gate also comes from Coducci via the Palazzo Corner as does the idea of rusticating the ground-floor façade. Heavy rustication was never popular in Venice until Longhena's day and the only comparable earlier example is the unfinished ground-floor rustication of the palace begun at San Samuel for Galeazzo Sforza. The triple-arched water entrance of Sansovino's Palazzo Corner is repeated at the Palazzo Pesaro, but the central opening is replaced with a wall and niche.

While these derivations are undeniable, the boldness of Longhena's

135. OVERLEAF LEFT The frescoed eighteenth-century ballroom of Ca' Rezzonico

136. OVERLEAF RIGHT Palazzo Pesaro: carved details by Baldassare Longhena

211

141. OVERLEAF LEFT *The Banquet of Cleopatra* – a fresco by Giambattista Tiepolo in the Palazzo Labia, c. 1745–50 (photo Scala)

142. OVERLEAF RIGHT Palazzo Labia with S. Geremia church and the Grand Canal

137. OPPOSITE The façade of Palazzo Pesaro on the Rio delle due Torri

138. RIGHT The corner of Palazzo Pesaro on the Grand Canal and the rio

139. BELOW LEFT A carved detail by Longhena on the Palazzo Pesaro façade

140. BELOW RIGHT Grotesque masks on the base of the Palazzo Pesaro

treatment of them remains remarkable. The rustication is cyclopean; a boldly carved if somewhat bizarre balustrade runs the entire width of the *piano nobile*; grotesque masks and heads jut out from the base of the building; and highly carved plumed, helmeted heads form the keystones of the window arches. The corner on the rio is brilliantly turned with a mass of indentations and superimpositions which confuse and intrigue the eye. The flatter rio façade is entirely of Istrian stone as well: one of the few examples of a palace with two finished façades. The more restrained treatment is to be ascribed to Gaspari, but Longhena's feeling for volume is barely suppressed. The courtyard is again a bold Baroque version of Sansovino's restrained exercise in classicism at the Palazzo Corner. An immense eighteenth-century staircase rises in two flights from the *andron* to the gigantic rooms of the *piano nobile* and continues to the upper floors.

The Pesaro of San Stae came to Venice from the Romagna in the mid-thirteenth century. They were early known as the Pesaro del Carro from their ownership of the carriage that provided portage for the barges of the Brenta river to the lagoon at Fusina. Later, after locks had been built, the Pesaro del Carro still owned and maintained the passage from the river to the lagoon. One of the most illustrious of the branch of San Stae was Jacopo, who as Bishop of Papho in Cyprus was appointed Apostolic Legate and general of the papal armies allied with Venice against the Turk. It was he who commissioned from Titian in 1519 the famous *pala*, or altarpiece of Ca' Pesaro, for the family altar at the Frari. Just as Jacopo represents the many military triumphs of the family as well as its enlightened patronage of the arts, Francesco's name is known in Venetian history as the one man on whom blame might be laid for the conquest of the Republic in 1797. Sent several times as ambassador to Napoleon, he refused the offer of an alliance between France and the Republic and staunchly upheld the Republic's neutrality. Since her neutrality had already been twice breached, by the Austrian army's retreat across her territories and by the French forces already encamped at Verona, it was an unrealistic position. Napoleon feared the Austrians might retrench or even attack, and his supply lines were stretched to the limit. At Leoben in Styria he simultaneously offered an armistice to the Austrians and declared war on the Venetians. The whole affair was ended in a matter of weeks. Years later in exile, Napoleon wrote that Pesaro's refusal of an alliance, which seemed then like temporizing until the Austrians could reinforce and attack, had forced him, a nervous young general, into his declaration of war.

The last of the Pesaro of San Stae was a certain Pietro, who emigrated to London where he sold over 200 paintings from the immense family collections. He died in London in 1830 and his heirs disposed of the rest of the house's contents. From the Pesaro the palace passed into the Gradenigo family and was then sold to the General Duke La Masa, whose widow bequeathed it to the city of Venice. In 1902 it became the city's Museum of Modern Art, housing the collection begun in 1897 with the prize-winning paintings of the first Venice Biennale.

143. Palazzo Pesaro, the masterpiece of Baldassare Longhena at San Stae

144. OVERLEAF LEFT The ballroom or *sala dei putti* of Palazzo Albrizzi

145. OVERLEAF RIGHT The *portego* of Palazzo Albrizzi

Palazzo Albrizzi

The Palazzo Albrizzi in the parish of Sant' Aponal is another of the Venetian palaces situated on one of the minor canals. The visitor who loses himself on foot would be well advised to seek the palace by gondola, for both the rio di San Cassiano and the rio della Madonnetta lead directly to it from the Grand Canal. The house was built in the sixteenth century for the Bonomo family and was bought from them in two stages by the Albrizzi in 1648 and 1692. It is of an extremely simple though imposing architecture with the popular Serlian group used as the principal element on the *piano nobile*. The palace is typical of the many important houses that were built in the interior of the city and in this case, as in others, a plain façade on both the rio and the campo masks an extraordinarily rich interior.

The handsome water-gate can still be lit by the magnificent *fanale da galera*, or stern lantern, of the galley of Venice's last great naval hero, Admiral Angelo Emo. The steep and narrow barrel-vaulted staircase rises in two flights to the splendid rooms of the *piano nobile*. Elaborate stucco-work of the late seventeenth century, attributed to Abbondio Stazio from the Ticino, makes a veritable ice palace of the walls and ceilings of the *portego*. Three openings were left in the ceilings and four ornate frames break up the side walls, designed for the insertion of gigantic canvases, which were, it seems, cut to fit Stazio's frames. These frames are the organizational unit of the decorative scheme with fronds, heavy draped cloths, cartouches and giant putti embellishing them. A lighter motif of vines, leaves, and flowers decorates the flatter surfaces. The richness of the *portego* stuccoes contrasts with the simpler, traditional design of the furniture – Rococo wooden-backed chairs and settees more for show than comfort.

But the plaster-work for which the Palazzo Albrizzi is famous is at its richest in the almost cubical ballroom or *sala dei putti*. The regular dimensions of the room are unusual in Venice, where the site generally imposed oblong shapes on the interior. And in fact the ballroom is part of an adjacent building – perhaps that purchased by the Albrizzi in 1692, which would also explain the apparently later date of the exuberant stucco-work. In the ballroom Stazio hid the original beamed ceiling behind rich stucco folds of a billowing canopy with twenty-eight putti holding up the great weight of the cloth. At the corners full-length male figures seated on the cornice strain like caryatids under the weight of rich folds of drapery. The plainer walls are a perfect complement to the rich ceiling and the whole is completed by a series of family portraits hung above consoles, whose friezes are carved with gilded portrait medallions of other members of the family. From the ballroom one proceeds to the Louis XVI atmosphere of a room lined with mirrors and still containing the handsome furniture designed for it. From this last room of the enfilade along the rio, a bridge crosses over the canal to a high-walled garden that was once the site of one of the city's numerous private theatres – the Teatro di San Cassiano, built in 1636, the first public opera house in Europe.

The Albrizzi, whose descendants still inhabit the palace, came from Bergamo in the seventeenth century. They had at various times been merchants in canvas and later in the Levantine trade in oil. For this latter enterprise they ran their own ships, which they offered to the Republic for the wars against the Turks. In 1661 they were inscribed as citizens of the Republic and in 1667, after donating 100,000 ducats to the Republic's war efforts in Crete, they were admitted to the ranks of the patriciate. The most noteworthy of their family was the poetess Isabella Albrizzi, who held a literary salon for the great of the day at her casinò near San Moisè. There she received Ugo Foscolo, Ippolito Pindemonte, Stendhal, who found her conversation fascinating, and Byron, who called her 'the de Stael of Venice'. Her friend the sculptor Antonio Canova carved for her a bust of Helen, which inspired Byron to a poem. The bust is in the house at Sant' Aponal as are other mementoes of Isabella's fame.

Apart from the magnificence of its decoration, the Palazzo Albrizzi is virtually unique in today's Venice as one of the last private houses lived in by one household and not divided into separate apartments and offices.

Palazzo Pisani

The Palazzo Pisani at campo Santo Stefano is a highly unusual building in terms of Venetian architectural conventions. Not only are its size, its block-like wings and its loggia-divided courtyard remarkable, but it is also one of the very few Venetian palaces whose campo façade was from the beginning as important as its canal façade. By the time the wings and the tall second floor were added, the campo façade had become the most important feature of the house. Had the Pisani's grandiose plans been carried out, a third façade would have been built on the Grand Canal as well. Only the Palazzo Labia suggests a parallel, but even there Venetian traditions determined the importance of the component parts – the rio façade is still the most important, and the so-called third façade of Palazzo Labia is merely a continuation of it, turning the corner as most architects had done when the side of a building was visible from the water.

The Pisani house is the work of several architects, and it was not until the early eighteenth century that the last major work was done on it. The ground and first floors are generally given to the architect of Palazzo Emo-Treves, Bartolomeo Monopola, and contemporary documents date his work there to 1614–15. However, it seems that some of his building collapsed in an earthquake in 1634. It was the Paduan architect Girolamo Frigimelica who gave the building its present shape in 1728 by adding the second floor. And between 1715 and 1740 the ballroom and library wing was added, closing the courtyard, which was then divided by the tall loggia-screen.

On the campo side as well as on the rio, the flat façades are entirely covered with *pietra d'Istria* and the *portego* windows are of the Papadopoli Serlian type, whereas the lateral windows are quite unusual. On either side of the central windows are three two-light windows, whose exceptional height is emphasized not only by the slender single column that divides the two round-arched lights, but also by the inset balustrades that lengthen the windows' base. The only projecting balcony is that of the *piano nobile portego* and its function in providing a focal point in the centre of a very wide façade is emphasized by the prominence of its supporting brackets. Despite its width and the disposition of the lateral windows, the basic plan of the Palazzo Pisani is conventionally Venetian. The *portego* and the *andron* run the short depth of the house to the rio and are not parallel to the façade as might be guessed from outside.

The courtyard, which opens off at right angles to the *andron*, is a long rectangle pointed in the direction of the Grand Canal. Half-way between the

146. The *andron* of Palazzo Albrizzi

147. Alessandro Vittoria's door-knocker at Palazzo Pisani

225

andron wing and the library wing it is divided by a four-storey screen, which consists of open arches on the ground floor, a closed corridor with pedimented windows above, and is crowned by two further floors of tall, open-arched loggias. The screen serves as a passageway between the long wings of the house and is only the width of a corridor. The motif is familiar to students of Italian palace architecture from the Palazzo Borghese in Rome, but in Venice it is unique and in essence – given the generally restricted building sites – very un-Venetian. There is every evidence that two wings similar in length to the long sides of the courtyards should have continued from the ballroom wing to the Grand Canal thus creating yet another courtyard between them, but the palace was never completed. It is said that the immense project was specifically forbidden by the government of the day. Judging from the scale of the Pisani villa at Strà, also being built by Frigimelica at this time, the Pisani had intended something colossal.

Undoubtedly the Pisani of Santo Stefano, unlike the Belloni at San Zan Degola, the Bon at San Barnaba, or the Venier at San Vio, could have afforded to realize their most ambitious projects. They were amongst the city's richest bankers and had pioneered the concept of the giro or transfer-bank at the Rialto in the fifteenth century, an idea taken over by the government's *Banco della Piazza*. The Santo Stefano branch was founded by one Alvise (1544–1622), whose father was of the branch of the family known as the Pisani del Banco. A sure indication of massive wealth in the later centuries of the Republic was the election of a member of a family as doge and in 1735 another Alvise of Santo Stefano was raised to the ducal dignity. The immense villa at Strà was commissioned to celebrate the beginning of his ducal reign.

But the splendour of the Pisani of Santo Stefano is better summarized in the career of Alvise I Almorò, ambassador and Knight of San Marco. In 1784 he personally entertained King Gustav III of Sweden to a banquet and festivities that became legendary for their magnificence. He also showed the enlightened monarch the treasures of the family and the library, which the family opened to the public two days a week. Almorò's learning and statecraft were so admired that even though he held no brief for those who sought to profit from the downfall of the Republic, he accepted election as a member of the provisional municipal government. In this capacity and as one of the city's richest men, he offered his house to the newly arrived viceroy, Eugène de Beauharnais, for his official entry into Venice. Beauharnais was responsible for the formation of the Academy picture gallery, taking over the secularized buildings of the convent of the Carità as well as the disbanded Scuola Grande attached to it, to house the paintings taken from deconsecrated Venetian churches. In 1807 Almorò Pisani was made president of the Accademia, a position first held, in 1756, by Giovanni Battista Tiepolo.

In 1818 the palace was divided between the heirs of Almorò and his brother. Some apartments in the library wing were let to artists, and it was from the window of one of these that the young Swiss painter Léopold Robert threw

148. The campo façade of the immense Palazzo Pisani at Santo Stefano

Palazzo Pisani

himself in despair over the unrequited love of Princess Carlotta Bonaparte in 1835. The last of the Pisani di Santo Stefano died in 1880 and between 1898 and 1916 parts of the divided palace were bought to house the Liceo Musicale, which in 1940 became the Benedetto Marcello Conservatoire. In 1940–2 the palace underwent extensive restoration, not only to render it practicable as a conservatoire, but also to remove the various accretions of nineteenth-century taste.

149. The eighteenth-century screen separating the two courtyards of Palazzo Pisani

Palazzo Venier dei Leoni

The Palazzo Venier dei Leoni on the Grand Canal is often mistaken for a modern building. Its long, low façade covered with vines and the fact that it houses the Peggy Guggenheim collection of modern art contribute to this impression. In fact, the original project for the palace was presented to the Venier family in 1749 by the architect Lorenzo Boschetti, but the building was never finished. Boschetti was a neo-Palladian architect whose church of San Barnaba with its giant Corinthian order shows the influence of the Vicentine master and of Giorgio Massari, the architect of the Palazzo Grassi and the church of the Gesuati. At the Palazzo Venier, however, Boschetti seems to have had in mind a building in the Longhena style. His project, which is known to us from engravings and from the unique survival of his wooden architect's model, would have been, along with the Palazzo Labia, the last palace built on such extravagant lines. No one seems certain as to why the building was never completed, but given the financial difficulties the Bon encountered in building Longhena's Palazzo Rezzonico, or the fifty-odd years it took the Pesaro to complete the house Longhena designed for them, it seems likely that the Venier simply ran out of money. From the model one can see that the Palazzo Venier would have been larger and more grandiose than either of Longhena's great palaces.

Even the little that was built of the Palazzo Venier indicates the scale Boschetti had in mind. The water-entrance stairs, which were an essential part of the largest houses, from Coducci's Vendramin or the Corner della Ca' Grande to the Rezzonico and Pesaro palaces, are here expanded into a high, raised terrace extending in front of the house; the ground-floor level is raised higher still. The height of this so-called ground floor is such that the Palazzo Venier is the only house in Venice with what might be called a basement – that is to say, a series of rooms under the ground floor, not of course underground, for in Venice that would mean under water.

The whole of the ground-floor façade is covered with *pietra d'Istria* rustication and is divided into sections by pilasters similar to Longhena's at Ca' Rezzonico. The triple opening of the water-gate is also Longhenesque in inspiration, but the model shows us that the whole would have surpassed even Longhena's most extravagant ideas. The columned atrium would have led to an enormous courtyard surrounded on all four sides by apartments of the palace – something seen on a much smaller scale only at the Grassi, Labia, and Rezzonico houses.

The Venier were among the most ancient of Venetian families. They traced

their descent from the *gens* Aurelia of Rome and in the service of the Republic they produced three doges, eighteen procurators of San Marco, and numerous captains general. Among the most renowned of their family was Sebastiano Venier, the hero of the great naval victory of the Venetian and allied fleets over the Turk at Lepanto in 1571. The Venier of San Vio originally owned a house which stood between the present Venier dei Leoni and the Palazzo Dario. It was called the Venier delle Toreselle from the towers which rose above the roofscape of Dorsoduro and which can be seen in some of Canaletto's paintings and engravings. This house, which had been divided several times until it was owned partly by the Donà delle Toreselle and partly by the Scuola di San Rocco, was torn down in the nineteenth century. The palace that had stood on the site of the Venier dei Leoni was a fifteenth-century Gothic house similar to the Palazzo Barbaro. The projected house to be built on the cleared site would have had the ground floor that survives, a mezzanine floor, and two *piani nobili* of the Rezzonico type with an attic above them. It seems that the house and the branch of the Venier family took their name from a lion that was brought to Venice in 1763 and was kept in the garden in the company of a number of small dogs. However, the giant lion's heads at the base of the façade could just as easily have provided the family and the house with the sobriquet.

After the fall of the Republic, the palace changed hands a number of times. At one point it was the guest-house of the Comtesse de la Baume-Pluvinel, who lived in the Palazzo Dario, and Henri de Régnier describes his stay there in his Venetian memoirs. Other foreign owners have lived there, including the colourful and eccentric Marchesa Casati. Since 1951 the house has been the property of Mrs Peggy Guggenheim, who generously opens it three times a week to visitors and to students of her remarkable collection of modern paintings and sculpture.

150. A view of the Grand Canal and the Salute from the Accademia bridge: the unfinished Venier dei Leoni is on the right, with Palazzo Dario

151. Palazzo Venier dei Leoni: lion heads facing the Grand Canal

Palazzo Labia

The palace of the Labia family in the parish of San Geremia was built in two stages. The principal, most highly decorated façade, which overlooks the rio di Cannaregio and is continued to the short corner façade towards the Grand Canal, was built in the Longhena style by Andrea Cominelli towards the end of the seventeenth century. The rear elevation on the campo San Geremia, in a simpler style, was completed around 1750 either by Alessandro Tremignon, the architect of the overcharged Baroque façade of San Moisè, or perhaps by his less well-known son, Paolo. The campo and rio façades summarize many of the distinctions between seventeenth- and eighteenth-century Venetian palace architecture. The campo façade, with its plain central *portego* opening and its low-relief handling of the Istrian stone rustication and overall facing, is an example of the generally conservative eighteenth-century taste widespread in Venice, but rarely associated with a particular architect. The rio and corner façades are executed in the richer vocabulary of Longhena's borrowings from several master architects of the Venetian tradition. The pilasters that break up the ground-floor walls at the Palazzo Labia derive from Coducci's Palazzo Loredan or Sanmicheli's Palazzo Grimani, where the mezzanine windows are set equally high; the highly sculptural combination of pilasters and rustication comes from Longhena's Ca' Rezzonico. Pilasters are used instead of columns on the floors above as well, though both in the rhythm of their distribution and in the carved decoration used with them they recall the work of Sansovino; the oval windows of the attic are a direct borrowing from that architect's Palazzo Corner. The most striking feature of this façade is the frieze with large high-relief heraldic eagles, which are tilted, as are the Longhenesque keystone masks, to be better seen from the water. The use of heraldic devices as frieze decoration goes back to Coducci's Palazzo Loredan and to the Lombardesque Palazzo Contarini-Polignac.

The other noteworthy feature of the Palazzo Labia's rio façade, besides its rich decoration, is its lack of symmetry by Venetian standards. Two quite separate developments in the building were responsible for this. First, Cominelli built an extension to the palace along the rio towards the Grand Canal. This provided the house with a ballroom, the usual reason for such enlargements in the seventeenth century. Only this one room was gained on the *piano nobile*, however, because the bell-tower of San Geremia stands against the rear wall of the room and thus obstructs expansion in that direction. Cominelli probably intended also an extension on the other side of the house to balance the one he built; for some unknown reason this was never

152. Rio di Cannaregio seen from the Grand Canal with the Church and the bell-tower of San Geremia, the side façade of Palazzo Labia and the bridge of the obelisk

153. A detail of the main façade of Palazzo Labia

carried out. On the campo side, however, the house was lengthened in the direction Cominelli had intended for the rio façade: this extension was part of the mid-eighteenth-century building. Curiously enough, this produced a lack of symmetry on the campo façade that is exactly the reverse of that on the rio.

A last peculiarity of the structure remains to be explained: one that contributed in part to the Palazzo Labia's reputation as one of the most important of Venetian eighteenth-century palaces. This was an alteration to the interior. The owners, baulked for some reason of their plan to extend the palace on the rio, decided to make a ballroom in the centre of the palace. This was achieved on the *piano nobile* by knocking the side room opposite the stair opening into what had been the *portego*. New walls were built so that a tall square room emerged from where the central section of the *portego* and a side room had originally been. The shape of the room is completely un-Venetian, just as the doors are placed with a symmetry not possible in the conventional Venetian plan. The new room was feasible only because the Labia could demolish adjacent buildings to clear a courtyard that would make a light-well for the room. Their unusual ballroom was then prepared for the most splendid decoration to be seen in Venice. The entire room was frescoed with the most subtle *trompe l'oeil* architecture designed by Gerolamo Mengozzi-Colonna. It not only confounds and delights the eye but also provides the most wonderful frame for some of the finest fresco work ever done by Giambattista Tiepolo. On one wall he depicted the legendary encounter of Antony and Cleopatra and on the opposite wall he painted Cleopatra's banquet. These spectacular and theatrical scenes are set in the costume of the Venetian Cinquecento and clearly illustrate Tiepolo's debt to Veronese, while the ceiling appears to open to reveal a celestial vision of cloud-borne deities and allegorical figures proclaiming the glory of the house of Labia.

The Labia were among the richest families of eighteenth-century Venice. Originally from Gerona in Spain, where their name was Lasbias, they had emigrated first to Avignon and then to Florence. They settled in Venice in the early seventeenth century and by 1646 they were admitted to the patriciate after the usual contribution of 100,000 ducats to the war effort in Crete. For the tourist today the site of their house seems far from the centre of the city, but in the days of the Republic, the rio di Cannareggio was not only a busy artery of the city's waterbound trade, but also the canal along which most of the ambassadors to Venice established their embassies and residences. The church of San Geremia was one of the oldest foundations in the city and the Labia palace was built on the site of ancient houses belonging to the Morosini and Malipiero, two of the oldest families of the Republic. ·

The Palazzo Labia has always been a byword for great riches and splendid festivities in Venice, from the days of the Labia who was supposed to have flung his gold plate from the windows during a dinner, proclaiming, 'O l'abbia o non l'abbia sono sempre Labia' (Have it, or have it not, I am always Labia), until the spectacular ball given there in the 1950s by Charles de Besteigui. After the much publicized auction of Besteigui's treasures in 1964 the building was bought by the R.A.I., the Italian Radio Television corporation, and from 1969 to 1972 underwent extensive restoration to convert it into their headquarters. It was an exemplary restoration and the palatial aspect of the *piano nobile* was successfully preserved, while the less significant apartments were converted to suit the requirements of an efficient modern business organization.

154. The narrow façade of Palazzo Labia visible from the Grand Canal

Palazzo Zenobio

The late seventeenth-century Palazzo Zenobio, which overlooks the rio dei Carmini in the *sestiere* of Dorsoduro, is a curious if not unique building in Venice. A few earlier Venetian palaces may seem to resemble it, like Coducci's stark, long Palazzo Zorzi at San Severo, the exceptionally elongated façade of the Loredan palace at Santo Stefano, or even the early seventeenth-century campo façade of Bartolomeo Monopola's Palazzo Pisani, but in essence Antonio Gaspari's design is very original by Venetian standards. Its stark, flat façade of *pietra d'Istria*, its exceptional width – seven central windows light the ballroom and there are four lateral windows on each side – and the use of undecorated rectangular windows on the secondary floor above the *piano nobile*, all herald the austerity of the neo-classical school and may even have provided the prototype for Andrea Tirali's cold, yet well-proportioned Palazzo Priuli-Manfrin built at least fifty years later. The traditional Venetian features employed by Gaspari here are the central Serlian window flanked by a pair of windows separated by double columns as at the Palazzo Balbi, and the round-arched windows with well-marked imposts so often used by Longhena. Otherwise the building seems a self-conscious reply to Longhena's exuberance, a not unnatural reaction from an architect who laboured for years to imitate his designs for the gigantic Palazzo Pesaro.

The impression of unrelieved starkness is somewhat misleading, for Gaspari intended a giant, elaborately carved shield of the Zenobio arms to be placed in the empty segmental arch of the attic storey. The arms were removed in the early nineteenth century but can still be seen in the garden. The garden of the Palazzo Zenobio was always one of its most famous features. An engraving by Carlevaris shows it laid out in formal parterres with Tommaso Temanza's eighteenth-century casinò as a backdrop. Casinò became a Venetian institution, especially in the eighteenth century, though few survive today. Originally they were small houses or pavilions set in gardens and used solely for dining and informal entertaining. In Venice the example best known to tourists is the Casinò degli Spiriti in the Contarini dal Zaffo gardens on the northern side of the city. By the eighteenth century these buildings still served for informal entertaining, but their decoration became more elaborate. Temanza's for the Zenobio has a ground floor with Ionic columns and statues in niches, and an upper floor which housed the family library and archive of more than 6,000 volumes. A balcony opened onto the floor below, an arrangement found not only in some other surviving casinò of Venice, but also in some of the city's older cafés.

155. Palazzo Zenobio, the late seventeenth-century building by Antonio Gaspari

Palazzo Zenobio

The Zenobio who lived at the Carmini came originally from Verona and were inscribed on the rolls of the patriciate in 1646. They were patrons of the arts and famous for their philanthropy. The Venetian view painter, Luca Carlevaris, lived in the house and was known to the Venetians as Luca di Ca' Zenobio. The last of the Zenobio, Alvise, left the city after the fall of the Republic and went to live in London. There he mastered the English language and wrote for the English papers of the day. Even though he was dejected by the collapse of Venice, he remained passionately interested in her future and was much praised by the provisional municipal government for his gift of one hundred sequins to be awarded for the best proposal for the revival of Venetian commerce. He died in London in 1815 and the house was inherited by his sister, Alba, the widow of one of the last procurators of the Republic, Alessandro Albrizzi. Also known for her munificence, she died in 1837 and her heirs sold the palace to a Count Salvi of Vicenza, who in 1844 began an extensive programme of restoration.

The result was the virtual disappearance of the magnificence that had once made the Palazzo Zenobio famous in the city, but the ballroom with its frescoes by Louis Dorigny was left untouched. In 1850 the palace was sold to a community of Armenian Catholic fathers, who still maintain a college for the education of Armenian boys there. In establishing themselves in Venice this congregation, founded only a few years before, in 1836, continued a tradition that stretched back to the thirteenth century. The Armenians had built their first church in Venice in the fifteenth century and later had a Scuola of their own, decorated with paintings by Carpaccio. Their dead were buried on the island of San Giorgio and their cemetery remained there until the sixteenth century, when the Palladian church was built over it.

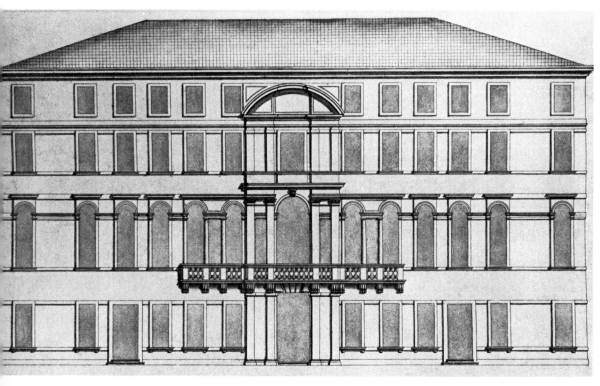

156. An engraving of Palazzo Zenobio (Visentini: *Venetian Palaces,* I, British Museum)

Palazzo Mangilli-Valmarana

The small eighteenth-century palace on the corner of the rio di Santissimi Apostoli and the Grand Canal, known to the Venetians as the Palazzo Mangilli-Valmarana, represents one of the most significant cultural links between Venice and England. For many years it was the home of George III's consular representative to the Most Serene Republic, Joseph Smith. The façade with its restrained neoclassical elements, now somewhat distorted by the later additions of the upper floors, is one result of that extraordinary collaboration between the British consul and his Venetian artist friends that so enriched the collections of eighteenth-century Englishmen. In 1743 Smith commissioned the engraver Antonio Visentini to design a new façade for this small Gothic house, which had once belonged to a branch of the Soranzo family. The work took an exceptionally long time, the façade not being unveiled until 1751.

The results of Smith's long life in Venice as a patron of the arts are almost all to be seen in England. Like his near-contemporaries in the consular service, Horace Mann at Florence and Sir William Hamilton at Naples, Joseph Smith combined diplomatic duties with an active business as a collector and dealer in the arts. He was a patron of Rosalba Carriera, the pastellist, of the Ricci family, and of many others, buying their works for his own collections or obtaining their paintings for Englishmen and their agents on the Grand Tour. But it was his patronage of Canaletto that most effectively influenced English taste in collecting. He commissioned Canaletto to paint the well-known series of views of Venice which he then asked Visentini to engrave. The engraver's dedication to Smith states clearly that the originals were in his house at SS. Apostoli. The views first appeared in 1742; Canaletto prepared further canvases for Visentini to engrave for a later edition, and the last version to appear in Smith's lifetime was published in 1751. Smith retired as consul in 1760 and in the same year, under financial pressure, he began to sell off his collection.

A great deal of mystery surrounds the exact disposal of the various Canalettos. We do not know with any precision which canvases came from Smith's own collections, which were commissioned from Canaletto through Smith, or which were second versions of Smith's paintings. In any case, the splendid collections of the Duke of Bedford, the Earl Fitzwilliam, and the Duke of Buckingham, the latter being now dispersed, were all connected with Smith in some way or another. We do know, however, that in the year of his retirement Smith sold the bulk of his private collection to the agents of

George III. There were fifty paintings and 140 drawings by Canaletto as well as items by other artists, including twelve overdoor paintings of English country houses by Visentini set in imaginary landscapes painted by Francesco Zuccarelli. Smith's library was also sold to George III and became the nucleus of the King's Library in the British Museum. Smith's interest in books led him to finance the Venetian publisher J. B. Pasquali, and together they reprinted Palladio's *Quattro Libri dell' Architettura,* thus providing a text-book for the eighteenth-century Palladian revival. Joseph Smith died in 1770 and was buried in the cemetery for Protestants founded by the Venetians as a special favour to James I. The cemetery no longer exists and consul Smith's bones rest in a common grave. Recently his tombstone was moved to the English church in the campo San Vio as a memorial to the Englishman who had done so much for the cultural relations between England and Venice.

Consul Smith's heirs sold the palazzo to a Count Gambara, from whom another patron of the arts, Count Giuseppe Mangilli, bought it in 1784. Mangilli commissioned the architect Antonio Selva to enlarge and redecorate the house. The next owner was also an important patron of the arts, Benedetto Valmarana of Vicenza. Since the early nineteenth century the house has been owned by descendants of the family who bought it from Valmarana, and Selva's neoclassical interiors have survived the taste of succeeding generations intact.

157. Palazzo Mangilli-Valmarana (left) and the church of SS. Apostoli

Palazzo Grassi

The palazzo of the Grassi family at San Samuel was built for them between 1748 and 1772 by Giorgio Massari. It is a well-proportioned building and seems almost consciously planned as a pendant to the Palazzo Rezzonico, which stands opposite on the Grand Canal and which Massari had completed to Longhena's designs. But at the Palazzo Grassi all trace of Longhenesque sculpturism and Baroque exuberance has disappeared, and a more restrained neoclassical mode is dominant: the orders are correctly Rustic, Ionic, and Corinthian. The ground floor is rusticated, it is true, but the rustication is flat and regular; the windows are virtually unadorned. The water-gate entrance is a variation on the Serlian motif of the Papadopoli house and the pedimented windows of the second *piano nobile*, set in compartments marked off by pilasters, can also be derived from Grigi's prototype. The lateral windows of the first *piano nobile* are reminiscent of the round-arched windows separated by doubled pilasters that Scamozzi had used at the Palazzo Contarini degli Scrigni. In fact, the entire building is conceived in the rather dry theoretical terms advocated by Palladio's disciple; everything is highly regular, well-proportioned, and as a result perhaps a bit dull.

The interior, on the other hand, is anything but dull. A four-columned

159. Looking across the court-yard to the water-gate of Palazzo Grassi

158. Palazzo Grassi at San Samuele, built between 1748 and 1772 by Giorgio Massari

atrium leads to a courtyard and straight on to a handsome grand staircase. The fine proportions of this ground-floor plan make it seem the only example in Venice where these otherwise un-Venetian elements are perfectly integrated into the house. The courtyard is now roofed over and the three elements, atrium, courtyard, and staircase, seem a single covered unit of the building. The staircase is an integral part of the plan, rising straight from the courtyard arcade and on an axis with the water-gate atrium opposite. It is housed in a *Treppenhaus* and at the level of the *piano nobile* is frescoed with a delightful crowd of carnival figures.

The Grassi family came from Bologna, but had settled at Chioggia as early as the thirteenth century. They were inscribed in the Silver Book as citizens of the Republic in 1646, but seem to have made their career in the service of the Church rather than the State. Five of them were bishops and the Grassi were delegated to entertain Pope Pius VI when he arrived at Chioggia before making his state entry into Venice. In 1718 Paolo Grassi was admitted to the patriciate after having contributed 60,000 silver ducats to the Venetian war against the Turks in the Morea. His son Angelo had the palace built.

By the late eighteenth century the wealth of the Grassi was conspicuous in a Venice where many patrician families were beginning to feel the effects of the State's diminished commerce with the East, the loss of her Levantine empire to the Turk, inflation, and the devaluation of the once impregnable ducat. The chroniclers of the day often mention the rich Grassi family. In 1779 they focused on the scandal of Margherita Condulmer Grassi, who threatened to leave her husband because he disapproved of her *cicisbeo*, the patrician Gaetano Dolfin. The *cicisbeo* was a widespread institution in eighteenth-century Italy. Generally a younger man, he was the patrician lady's escort to balls, to the opera, and in Venice also to the state-supervised gambling house called the Ridotto. He was not according to the conventions of the day her lover, though with Margherita Grassi there seems to have been some question in her husband's mind. In any case the scandal was peaceably resolved, though her husband seems to have been considered something of a ridiculous figure by his contemporaries for objecting to his wife's behaviour.

The Grassi died out in the early nineteenth century and the house then changed hands several times. At one time it was owned by an entrepreneur called Francesco degli Antoni, who earned the encomiums of his contemporaries by installing public baths near the house. This modern marvel was equipped in Pompeian fashion with hot and cold, fresh and salt water, as well as mud-baths. The water was drawn, it seems, through an elaborate system of tubing from the nearby Grand Canal. Later in the century the Palazzo Grassi was converted into a hotel and still later it was bought by a Greek, who was responsible for the first extensive restorations. In 1951 it became the seat of the International Centre for the Study of the Arts and Costume and has been the setting for numerous important exhibitions. An open-air theatre was built in the garden and part of the Biennale's programme of drama took place there.

Palazzo Treves

The last of the palaces included in this study is out of chronological order. It was probably built for a branch of the Corner family by Bartolomeo Monopola, the architect of part of the Palazzo Pisani at Santo Stefano, sometime in the seventeenth century. Neither the date nor the attribution need concern us here, for the architecture of its Grand Canal façade is rather conventional. The long rio façade is more interesting with its Serlian windows, the grouping of rectangular openings on all floors, and the false mezzanine windows between the first and second *piano nobile*.

160. The Canova room at Palazzo Treves with the statues of Hercules and Ajax

Unprepossessing as the prospect on the Grand Canal appears, the house has an extremely fine interior. This contrast between the exterior appearance of a Venetian palace and its interior is not unique to the Palazzo Treves. In fact, it is just this contrast that makes the Palazzo Treves representative of a great number of Venetian palaces which have not been included in a study planned to show the developments and peculiarities of Venetian palace architecture. The interior also merits inclusion here for another reason. It is virtually the only example of Venetian interior decoration after the fall of the Republic.

The house was bought by the barons Treves de' Bonfili in 1827 from the Emo family, who had inherited it from the Corner. The Treves were bankers to the Austrian empire and were held in such high esteem by the Imperial court that they were not only ennobled but also designated as *hoffähig*, i.e. having entrée to the Viennese court. Shortly after their purchase of the house, the Treves set about redecorating in the fashion of the early nineteenth century. Structurally they altered little, merely joining the house to an adjacent building and adding the requisite staircase hall at the back of the *sala del portego*. Because they conserved the essential plan, unlike so many who redecorated their houses later in the nineteenth century, the Palazzo Treves is still a very Venetian house and it still contains a number of specifically Venetian features such as the *liagò* or enclosed balconies.

The *piano nobile* apartments are mostly furnished in the style known as Charles X, rich in the use of fine mahogany, ebony, and rosewood, but generally slightly heavier and more curvilinear than the elaborate ormolu-mounted creations of the first Empire. The frescoes, friezes, and ceiling decorations are in the neoclassical style and a fine collection of paintings illustrates the work of early nineteenth-century Italian artists. There are also interesting occasional paintings such as a depiction of the return of San Marco's golden horses from France as a result of the second Treaty of Paris.

On the mezzanine floor of the adjacent house the Treves had a special columned hall designed to house the giant statues of Hector and Ajax sculpted by the fashionable Antonio Canova. These attracted much admiration, and on an easel nearby stands a keyed painting of the visit of Emperor Francis II and Metternich to inspect the Treves collections. The house, still beautifully maintained by a descendant of the bankers who bought and redecorated it, continues to represent the hidden treasures of many of the palaces of Venice.

161. Palazzo Treves on the Grand Canal and the rio di San Moisè

Select Bibliography

L. ANGELLINI, *Le opere in Venezia di Mauro Coducci*, Milan 1945

E. ARSLAN, *Gothic Architecture in Venice*, London 1972

E. BASSI, *Architettura del Sei e Settecento a Venezia*, Naples 1962

— *Palazzi di Venezia, Admiranda Urbis Venetae*, Venice 1976

J. C. DAVIS, *The Decline of the Venetian Nobility as a Ruling Class*, Baltimore 1962

G. FONTANA, *Venezia Monumentale: I Palazzi*, Venice 1845–63

— *Cento palazzi di Venezia storicamente illustrati*, Venice 1865

R. GALLO, *I Pisani ed i palazzi di Santo Stefano e di Stra*, Venice 1960

P. GAZZOLA, *Michele Sanmichele*, Venice 1960

D. HOWARD, *Jacopo Sansovino*, London 1975

J. R. HALE (ed.), *Renaissance Venice*, London 1972

F. C. LANE, *Venice: a Maritime Republic*, London 1973

— *Venice and History*, Baltimore 1966

O. LOGAN, *Culture and Society in Venice 1470–1790*, London 1972

G. LORENZETTI, *Venice and Its Lagoon*, Rome 1961

M. LUYTENS (ed.), *Effie in Venice*, London 1965

G. MARIACHER, *Il palazzo Vendramin-Calergi*, Milan 1950

P. MOLMENTI, *La storia di Venezia nella vita privata*, Bergamo 1905–8

J. J. NORWICH, *Venice: The Rise to Empire*, London 1977

T. OKEY, *The Old Venetian Palaces and the Old Venetian Folk*, London 1907

D. R. PAOLILLO AND C. DALLA SANTA, *Il Palazzo Dolfin-Manin a Rialto*, Venice 1970

B. PULLAN, *Rich and Poor in Renaissance Venice*, Oxford 1971

L. PUPPI, *Michele Sanmichele*, Padua 1971

J. RUSKIN, *The Stones of Venice*, London 1851–3

G. SCATTOLIN, *Le case fondaco sul Canal Grande*, Venice 1961

C. SEMENZATO, *L'architettura di Baldassare Longhena*, Padua 1954

G. TASSINI, *Alcuni palazzi ed antichi edifici di Venezia*, Venice 1879

— *Curiosita Veneziane*, Venice 1913

TOURING CLUB ITALIANO, *Venezia e dintorni*, Rome 1971

E. R. TRINCINATO, *Venezia Minore*, Milan 1948

UNESCO, *Rapporto su Venezia*, Milan 1969

C. YRIARTE, *La roie d'un patricien de Venise au 16e siecle*, Paris 1874

A. ZORZI, *Venezia Scomparsa*, Milan 1971

162. The Grand Canal during the gondola races of the September regatta from Palazzo Martinengo to the bell-tower of San Bartolomeo at the Rialto

Glossary

Acqua alta: the exceptionally high water, resembling a tide, which
               floods Venice

Altana: the wooden roof-top platforms used as terraces or for
               drying and airing carpets and linen

Andron: the ground-floor hall behind the water-gate entrance of a
               Venetian house or palace

Arsenalotti: the workers of the Venetian state shipyard

Arsenale: the ship-building and fitting yards, as well as the armament
               depot of the Republic

Bailo: the resident Venetian ambassador at Constantinople, the
               Republic's most important embassy

Bucintoro: the hundred-oared ceremonial barge of the doge

Calle: the Venetian street

Campo: the Venetian town square

Casa or Ca':   the Italian for house; used in abbreviated form in Venice to
               designate a palace
               Casa d'affitto: a house or palace let by the owners
               Casa domenicale: the principal house of a branch of a
                   patrician family
               Casa di stazio: a house resided in by the owners
               Casa fondaco: the early Venetian combination of a residence
                   and a place of business

Casinò: a garden pavilion for informal entertaining

Cicisbeo: a lady's escort or chevalier servant

Colleganze: the joint venture partnerships common in Venetian
               commerce and finance

Compagnia delle calze: a company of the hose, a club of young nobles
               identified by their parti-coloured hose

Consiglieri ducali: the six councillors of the doge

Consiglio dei dieci: the Council of Ten

Cortile: a courtyard

Curia: an arcade of columns extending the width of the main
               block, both on the ground and first floors, of a Veneto-
               Byzantine palace

Doge: the chief officer or duke of the Venetian Republic; elected
               for life

Dominante: the description of Venice referring to her dominant role
               over the cities and territories of the Republic

250

Fanale: a lantern from the stern of a galley

Fondamenta: a quay-like walkway along a canal

Fondamente nuove: the sixteenth-century promenade built on the northern edge of the city

Intonaco: the plaster surfacing of a wall

Inquisitorii di stato: the state inquisitors; a civil office not to be confused with the Holy Office or Roman Inquisition

Liagò: a roofed terrace; later an enclosed projecting balcony

Libro d'Oro: the registry of the Venetian patriciate begun in 1297
Libro d'argento: the registry of the Venetian *cittadini originarii* or citizen class

Maggior Consiglio: the Great Council or lower house of the Venetian Parliament

Marciana: the state Library of St Mark housed in a building by Sansovino on the Piazzetta

Marmorino: marble dust mixed and applied like paint to counterfeit marble slabs

Morea: the Venetian name for the Peloponnese

Palazzo: a designation used in Venice only for the Doge's Palace

Pali: the larch pilings driven as foundations for Venetian buildings or, secondarily, mooring poles painted with the house colours

Patera, Paterae: a flat stone plaque or ornament carved in bas-relief

Pergoli: Venetian dialect name for balconies

Piano nobile, piani nobili: the noble or principal floor of a Venetian house; generally the first full floor above the ground floor

Piazza: in Venice used only for the piazza di San Marco, St Mark's Square

Pietra d'Istria: Istrian stone, a white marble quarried in Istria

Pluteus, plutei: a marble panel placed between columns, often carved in bas-relief

Portego, porteghi: the central gallery-like hall of a Venetian house

Procurator: state administrators elected for life; originally three in number, later nine, they lived in the Procuratie Nuove on the south side of the Piazza

Promissione Ducale: a list of promises compiled by committee on the doge's death and sworn to by his successor

Provveditor: a high colonial and military administrative office, something like a military governor

Quarantia Criminal: the high criminal court of the Republic

Rio: the Venetian name for a canal, excepting the Grand Canal

Riva: a shore or bank, later paved and generally wider than a *fondamenta*

Sansovino, alla: a Venetian term for painted beam ceilings of a late fifteenth- or early sixteenth-century type

Savio, Savii:	the 'wise men' of the Republic, elected for a short term and comprising a privy council for the doge
Scrutinio:	the scrutiny or process of election for Venetian office; often specifically the ducal election
Scuola:	lay confraternities of the devout engaged in charitable works
Senatori:	the senators, sometimes called the Pregadi, members of the upper house of the Venetian parliament; elected from the Great Council
Sensa:	the feast of the Ascension, the principal feast of the Venetian civic calendar
Serenissima:	Most Serene, a title first bestowed on the ducal office by the Pope and then popularly extended to describe the Venetian Republic
Serliana:	a three-light opening, the central of which is surmounted by a round arch; the flanking openings have flat lintels or entablature; from the sixteenth-century architectural theoretician, Sebastiano Serlio
Sestiere:	one of the six administrative sections into which Venice is divided
Sottoportego:	a public passageway beneath a building; occasionally with an arcade along a *rio*
Terrazzo:	flooring made of crushed marble fragments laid in a brick powder paste
Terrafirma:	the mainland provinces of the Republic
Torreselle:	the flanking towers of a Veneto–Byzantine palace
Treppenhaus:	a building made specifically to house a staircase
Two/three-light window:	a window opening divided into two or three sections
Vera da pozzo:	a well-head
Volta del canal:	the bend in the Grand Canal where the flow changes from a southerly to an easterly direction

Index

Index